Smart Guide™
to
Managing Your Time

D1402146

About Smart Guides™

Welcome to Smart Guides. Each Smart Guide is created as a written conversation with a learned friend; a skilled and knowledgeable author guides you through the basics of the subject, selecting the most important points and skipping over anything that's not essential. Along the way, you'll also find smart inside tips and strategies that distinguish this from other books on the topic.

Within each chapter you'll find a number of recurring features to help you find your way through the information and put it to work for you. Here are the user-friendly elements you'll encounter and what they mean:

One of the main objectives of the *Smart Guide to Managing Your Time* is

The Keys
Each chapter opens by highlighting in overview style the most important concepts in the pages that follow.

Smart Money
Here's where you will learn opinions and recommendations from experts and professionals in the field.

Street Smarts
This feature presents smart ways in which people have dealt with related issues and shares their secrets for success.

Smart Sources
Each of these sidebars points the way to more and authoritative information on the topic, from organizations, corporations, publications, Web sites, and more.

Smart Definition
Terminology and key concepts essential to your mastering the subject matter are clearly explained in this feature.

F.Y.I.
Related facts, statistics, and quick points of interest are noted here.

What Matters, What Doesn't
Part of learning something new involves distinguishing the most relevant information from conventional wisdom or myth. This feature helps focus your attention on what really matters.

The Bottom Line
The conclusion to each chapter, here is where the lessons learned in each section are summarized so you can revisit the most essential information of the text.

not only to better inform you how you currently spend your time but also to teach you how to arrange your schedule and manage your life so you have more time to do the things you love.

Smart Guide™

to

Managing Your Time

Lisa Rogak

CADER BOOKS

John Wiley & Sons, Inc.

New York • Chichester • Weinheim • Brisbane • Singapore • Toronto

ISBN 0-471-31886-8

Printed in the United States of America

10 9 8 7 6 5 4 3 2 1

To Pennaman and Beast,
two cats who make valiant attempts
to manage my time for me
each and every day.

Acknowledgments

Sometimes the most effective methods of time management are the ones that are thrust upon you.

First of all, thanks should go to my laptop, which enables me to write anywhere and everywhere.

Next, I cannot forget to thank Shelly Yusko, who pokes and prods my carpal-tunnel-syndrome-ridden arms back to some semblance of working order when I spend way too much time on my laptop.

Lastly, I'd like to thank New Hampshire Electric Coop for allowing me to take a break from work with its frequent power outages, and my cats for rendering the battery for my laptop entirely useless by using it as a teething ring.

Contents

Introduction

So you say that your life feels so out of control that you have to take drastic measures or else you'll sell all your stuff, quit your job, and live out the rest of your days in peaceful but boring nothingness. You don't really want to go that far, do you?

Probably not, though simplifying your life to the extent that you would no longer have to worry about managing your time or organizing your space is appealing. If you could only take the best parts of this ultra-scaled-down lifestyle and apply it to your current overscheduled, messy existence, well then, you might experience peace and order without having to become a hermit.

Consider it done. By picking up this guide you have already begun to reverse the frenzied course that your life has been on. By reading these words, you've prevented the chaos from engulfing you further. Indeed, simply recognizing that your runaway train of a life doesn't work and, in fact, hasn't worked for years may already have motivated you to perform your everyday tasks a little bit differently just so you can feel like you have a little bit more control.

But there are lots of other things you can do to switch your life from the express track to the local track without worrying about accomplishing less in your life. And you'll learn about hundreds of them—some easy to do, others that will take a little bit of time and training to apply—in the *Smart Guide to Managing Your Time*.

You'll start by analyzing the variety of ways in which you tend to waste time and in which our speeded-up society actually encourages you to mismanage your time. Then you'll begin to learn how a few surprisingly simple changes can have a huge effect on your daily schedule. You'll learn about the interruptions you can control—as well as the ones you can't—and you'll be introduced to tools and organizers that can help you to get out from under your chaotic schedule and workspace.

You'll also discover the best ways to get others to go along with your plan—both at work and at home. And finally, you'll get a glimpse of a few ways you can start to make your dreams come true once you've freed up enough time to spend a while thinking about them.

I've always thought it would make an interesting study to find out how much more work the average person is responsible for, now that we've pretty much incorporated all the up-to-the-minute time-saving tools into our lives.

Is it 50 percent more? One hundred percent more? Or, if you're that average person, do you think you're performing the same amount of work that it once took five people to accomplish?

Of course, some days it could feel as if you are doing the work of a hundred people and as if you are the only one in charge of controlling a runaway train. Regardless of how you feel, it may seem as though you don't have the time to learn how you can better organize your time. When you feel like this, you should ask yourself if you have the time to continue on your current ragged path, where your schedule is running you and not the other way around.

Once you get your runaway train under control, there's no end to the number of things you can accomplish. But there's only one way to start, and that's by turning the page now, while you're thinking about it.

Where Does the Time Go?

THE KEYS

• You shouldn't feel guilty because it seems like you never have enough time to do everything you want to do; everyone's in the same boat.

• Technology has contributed to our hurried-up world by making you feel compelled to work longer hours and to respond to every beep and chirp.

• Many of the ways in which we waste time take up little time; it is their cumulative effect that hurts so much.

• Working at breakneck speed is a well-entrenched tradition in many societies, especially contemporary North America: you've probably been at it since childhood.

• It will help to discover what kind of time waster you are.

• You should strive to see both the forest and the trees when it comes to managing time and projects.

If they can put a man on the moon and clone a sheep, they should be able to create more hours in each day, right?

Unfortunately, it doesn't quite work that way. The early pundits of high technology optimistically predicted that due to scientific progress, human beings would have many more hours each week to spend on leisure pursuits because the robots, computers, and other technological wonders would pick up the slack. While this made sense in theory, what's happened in fact is that most of us are doing easily twice the work of our predecessors, with workloads that seem never to end. While computers have undoubtedly made your life more efficient, they have also provided a great excuse to cram more responsibilities into every minute of every day, just because you can. At the same time, however, they do nothing to prevent you from feeling anxious, overwhelmed, and out of breath as you muddle through your increasingly overscheduled days and nights.

The fact that you've picked up the *Smart Guide to Managing Your Time* means that you instinctively know that it is possible to get more done in less time without becoming a basket case; you just need to learn how. Thankfully, instead of waiting for science to create the thirty-six-hour day, you've already taken the first step toward making the most of the hours you actually have.

Why You Don't Have Enough Time

If you feel as though you're always running at least several steps behind, and never able to completely cross everything off your crumpled and disorganized to-do list, you're in good company. Between work, family, and community responsibilities, most people today feel they'll never be able to catch up and accomplish everything they want to do. And most of them feel guilty because they think they should be able to control their own hectic schedules.

Of course, since the days of the Pilgrims, Americans have been known for their strong work ethic, and in recent generations, for their propensity for workaholism. But while your great-grandparents may have worked from dawn to dusk to keep the farm going and the family fed, their list of chores was usually completed before sundown. Today, in this 24/7 world, stopping work at sundown seems like an absolute luxury for most of us.

People living on the cusp of the twenty-first century are constantly haunted by the thought that there will always be more to do than time to do it; indeed, many people take on new tasks without thinking about how they're going to find the time to get them done. You've probably heard the adage, "If you want something done, give it to a busy person." The chances are that if this busy person gets the work done when she says it will be done, she is not superwoman. She's probably as overwhelmed as you are; the difference is that she knows how to effectively manage her time through a combination of scheduling, organization, and delegation. In other words, she probably has a great filing system and more than likely hires someone to clean her house, among other effective time-management tools.

In recent surveys, when people were asked whether they would want their boss to reward them with more money or more time for a job well done, the obviously overwhelmed majority said they would choose to have more time. Unfortunately, for most overworked employees, being rewarded with extra time is pure fantasy, since they think they would have to take a less challenging job in order to gain it. Besides, few people actually have enough time to think about what they would do if they had more time, and they assume that their bosses would probably rather reward them with money instead of time away from a busy office.

How did we arrive at this particular point in time, where cell phones are used as a time management tool ("I don't have the time to return phone calls," is a frequent rationalization) and most of the people you know would love to have at least a couple of hours for themselves each day?

One reason for our harried lives is the sheer number of choices that exist today. Every second of every day, we are asked to choose how we're going to spend our time. And since so many of the choices sound very appealing, we tend to take on more than we have time to reasonably accomplish.

Because of these innumerable choices and the habits that we've developed around them, people have grown increasingly uncomfortable with having free time to just stare out the window, to go for a walk without any aerobic or performance-oriented goals in mind, or to just sit at the playground and watch the kids play on the monkey bars. Ours is an accomplishment-oriented society, where mothers who stay at home even part-time are looked down upon because the common belief is they're not doing anything. What it comes down to is that we are so used to having our days overscheduled and overbooked to a fault, we are afraid to have any unscheduled time; and when a gap looms, many people rush to fill it up as quickly as possible.

Another reason why you feel you don't have enough time is the crippling onslaught of information that crosses your path every day, along with the fact that you feel you need to keep up to date with it, not only for your career, but in order to help your family become healthier and happier or improve themselves in some other way. Out of the thousands of pieces of news and information you come across in the course of a week, there will be at least a few that will stand out enough for you to notice, and then there will be a few more that you feel compelled to notice. Before you realize what has happened, you've added another item to your to-do list. When you stop to consider how adding one more new task to your to-do list each day will affect your schedule, it's no wonder you feel there aren't enough hours in the day.

The good news is that you will see a noticeable difference in your schedule if you cross at least one thing off your to-do list every day. You'll learn how to do this, along with other time-saving and sanity-saving tips as you continue to read this book.

STREET SMARTS

It's never too late to start managing your time more effectively so that you gain the time to do the things that you want to do.

Besides Grandma Moses, who only began to use her prodigious talent when she was in her seventies, James Michener was a late starter who wrote his first novel when he was forty-two. One of his most often quoted lines of advice warns erstwhile time misman-agement experts that there's no excuse for postponing favorite tasks any longer:

"Don't put off for tomorrow what you can do today, because if you enjoy it today you can do it again tomorrow."

SMART MONEY

Some people are addicted to having the latest, greatest, fastest pieces of high-tech equipment, buying up the newest just because it's new. Management consultant and author Peter Drucker advises against this knee-jerk reaction.

He advises that when the time comes to consider replacing an old tool—whether pen and ink or a hand-held solar calculator—with a new counterpart, it only makes sense if the new item offers at least ten times the benefits of the old. Think about this the next time a speedier computer chip or a supposedly more efficient automobile appears on the market.

The Curse of Technology

The thousands of ads you've seen for fax machines, answering machines, e-mail software, and computers—in fact any piece of high-tech equipment—all have one thing in common: they promise to make your life run more easily and more smoothly. And indeed they do—at least after the initial learning curve, which always takes up more time than you initially planned. The magic these machines perform can work wonders to help you get twice as much done, usually in much less than half the time it would take without the equipment. For instance, in the time it would take to type one letter on an electric typewriter, a high-powered computer, laser printer, and powerful word-processing and database software will allow you to produce a hundred or more individually addressed letters, even with corresponding envelopes.

This speed and efficiency has obviously been the reason why we've been so enamored of technology. However, instead of viewing the time saved as time to be applied toward personal time, most people fill up the extra hours with more work. As a result, the amount of work they accomplish is incredible, and workplaces everywhere are filled with Supermen and Superwomen. Everything is fine—that is, until your computer goes down or your printer stops working. Then, the anxiety that develops from doing nothing—as well as from the idea of being so beholden to an amalgam of plastic, wires, and silicon—can drive your stress levels straight through the roof. Your boss starts clamoring for the work, which makes you start to look bad, then your blood pressure goes up even more, and so on.

Some of the new technological devices that have been introduced in the 1980s and 1990s have been nothing short of miraculous. Imagine a tool that lets you see who's calling before you pick up the phone, or a device that will vibrate against your hip to let you know when someone is calling you and you just happen to be miles away from the office. Twenty years ago, these inventions were found only in science fiction novels. Today, they're indispensable tools.

This is all well and good, but all of these technological wonders tend to assign the same level of urgency to each incoming message, which places an insidious drain on your time (and patience). When they beckon you, it's usually necessary to interrupt what you're doing to see who's trying to get in touch with you. These hidden time wasters may initially appear to be freeing up your time, but they're actually robbing Peter to pay Paul, which then contributes to the feeling that you're living in an eternal time debt. Cell phones certainly have their benefits when it comes to security and accessibility, but the fact that many commuter railroads and public transportation systems either limit the amount of time a commuter can spend on the phone or ban them altogether in certain areas is a testament to the fact that many people are becoming dissatisfied with the idea that we must always be tied to a cellular lifeline. Let's face it: no one is *that* indispensable.

While these high-tech devices are extremely useful and, in the case of e-mail, can save users thousands of dollars and minutes by making direct lines of communication possible, the downside is that we end up feeling like we're always in one big hurry, and that everything needs to be done yesterday, or else.

Well, guess what? The sky won't fall down and chances are you won't lose your job or income if you occasionally eschew speed for substance. In fact, slowing down once in awhile—which is covered in depth in chapter 8—may help you to gain perspective on the fast-paced path it seems that most people are traveling on these days. A 33 rpm perspective in a 78 rpm world can actually be quite amusing and educational. Just think of the insight a teetotaling designated driver gains into human nature when surrounded by a roomful of imbibers. Once you begin to manage your time better, and actually have some to spare, you'll look around at your less-enlightened colleagues and marvel that you used to be the same way.

Time Bandits

Besides technology and our great information glut, there's another reason why so many of us feel that our days just run away from us. Surprisingly, it's not the big, obvious time wasters that consume hours at a time. Instead, it's the cumulative effect if all the little ones we usually don't notice.

If you've ever read a book on how to keep a budget, the first thing the author may have suggested you do is to keep a written record of every penny you spend in the course of a day, from a quarter for the daily newspaper to the five bucks you spent on lunch. Taken by themselves, these expenditures don't seem like they should make much of a dent in your monthly budget. However, once you add up all those "insignificant" expenses, you'll see that they do amount to a sizable chunk of your budget. Once you know where your money goes, you can take steps to alter the way you spend it.

The same idea is true when it comes to small time wasters. Five minutes here and ten minutes there are not much by themselves. But once you add them all up, you'll probably be surprised at how much time slips away from your day—lost to inefficient scheduling, poor planning, or chatting with a friend or coworker and losing track of the time—making you late for your next meeting or deadline, and aggravating the feeling that you're forever stuck playing catch-up.

Here, then, are four of the most common ways in which we waste our time. How many have you been guilty of today?

Putting Off the Bad Stuff

Each of us has at least one daunting task—like giving a cat a pill or weeding the garden—that we endlessly postpone because (a) it hasn't reached the crisis point yet, and/or (b) it's so unpleasant that we can think of at least ten other chores that need our immediate attention. The problem with this brand of procrastination is that in most cases, the unpleasant chore simply doesn't go away,. In fact, these postponements are frequently like a leftover casserole you weren't crazy about: it sits in the refrigerator, eventually working its way to the back, where you know it's still there, but by that time it's gotten so old that you don't even remember what it was. And since you know that it's not going to be a pleasant experience to put it out of its misery, it sits there still, months after it should have been dealt with.

SMART SOURCES

Ever wonder how a slower pace of life would affect your life? It's easy to go online and research your "fantasy" life. Have you always wanted to learn how to build your own home? Visit the Shelter Institute or YesterMorrow to learn how you can take weekend or evening classes, and then build your own home on a part-time basis. Or if you want to pursue a college degree but don't have the time or live too far from a university, you can earn a degree through distance education. Go to Dogpile, a search engine that combs through eleven other search engines at once, and start your research by typing in "Distance Education" Or type in your own for a wealth of choices.

www.shelterinstitute.com

www.yestermorrow.org

www.dogpile.com

F.Y.I.

Using your time inefficiently not only fritters away valuable minutes and hours that are lost forever, but it can also be a real burden on your finances.

Think of all the things that cost you extra money due to sloppy time management: bounced check fees because you didn't take the time to balance your checkbook, and late fees because you didn't get around to returning your library books on time. Or maybe you scrimp and save, watching your nickels and dimes with a hawk's eye, only to blow your budget when you lose track of time, miss dinner, discover your refrigerator is empty, and the only place open is an expensive restaurant, so you have no choice.

Keep that famous old saying in mind: Time *is* money.

Unclear Goals

Whether it's an MBA that serves as your pot of gold at the end of a road filled with lots of hard work, or the desire to read at least one chapter in that new novel you bought three months ago but haven't made the time to even crack open, having a goal in sight is a great motivator. The time-management problem arises when you set a goal without having a game plan for how you will get there, which is particularly challenging if you feel you don't have enough time in your day as it is.

Too Many Interruptions

Unless you're a hermit, you probably have to deal with at least a few interruptions every day. Some may present an excuse to take a well-deserved break—especially if you're not inclined to take one when you need it—while you may welcome or even search out others because you don't like what you're working on. When it comes to the latter, an interruption can turn into procrastination, which can end up throwing off your entire day's schedule.

Aimless Daydreaming

Do you ever get lost in thought while staring out the window at nothing, and then the next time you look at the clock, almost an hour has gone by? Everybody needs some downtime during the day: taking a break is a great way to recharge your batteries and refresh your mind after a particularly long and stressful bout of work, whether you're at home or in the office. But if you're zoning out by surfing the web or flipping through the pages of a magazine and you're not really seeing the words and images that are passing before your eyes, you may be using your break as a way to escape from feeling overwhelmed. And unless you address the main cause of your stress, that feeling of being overwhelmed will only increase.

As is the case with any desire to change, the first step to managing your time more effectively is to become aware of the various bandits that rob you of your time. The biggest paradox is that since many of these time bandits come about as a direct result of working too hard and for too long without a break, the easiest way to rid your life of the ruthless thieves is to begin taking regular breaks. More on that in chapter 3.

Hurry Up and Wait

Humans, especially those who live in the so-called developed nations, are among the most impatient creatures on earth. Whether it's tailgating the car ahead of us because we're late for work or sticking a frozen solid pint of ice cream in the microwave because we find it unbearably long to wait the ten minutes it would take for the stuff to soften, when we want something, we want it now, and that's all there is to it.

To some extent, our need-it-done-yesterday philosophy is not entirely our fault. From babyhood, speed in all things is encouraged. Taking the time necessary to accomplish a task—while learning the right and wrong ways to do it—is largely frowned upon. Think about it: how many times have you seen an impatient mother tap her foot in the supermarket while her toddler chooses between the many different brightly colored boxes of cereal, picking up each one, shaking it, staring at the colors, all in an effort to fully experience it? After just a few minutes of this, the mother is completely out of patience and simply grabs a box, any box, from the shelf and tosses it into the shopping cart. She has, in effect, just punished her son for taking too long.

This scenario is repeated in classrooms and playgrounds as the child gets older, with time limits on tests and homework, even sports. Kids who are naturally programmed to move and think just a little more slowly than their classmates are penalized with lower grades as well as taunts from their peers. Since higher education places such a premium on students living a well-rounded life—attending classes, working a part-time job, and participating in extracurricular activities, without any thought of the time it takes to fit all of it in—the pace doesn't let up.

Adults have learned this lesson all too well, it seems. Time is of the essence in businesses of all shapes and sizes, where the faster you accomplish a task the more work you are considered capable of handling and the more gets piled onto your already oppressive workload. This madness of rewarding the accomplishment of work with even more work is the rule. Even after putting in a full day's work, the busy-ness doesn't stop, as many people bring work home or attend networking meetings and business dinners, often five nights a week.

After being indoctrinated for so many years about the importance of keeping up, it's hard to let go. The result is that many people spend their lives spinning around like the Tasmanian Devil and when they look back on what they have accomplished, all they can see is a lot of running around, the supersize bottles of antacid, and the regret that while they may have wanted to slow down, even when they tried, they found it emotionally and physically difficult to shift gears.

One sad byproduct of this hurried but all-too-common lifestyle is that something usually has to give, and often the first things to go are personal relationships and your health, not to mention your happiness. And once those are gone, all the money—or time, for that matter—in the world won't get them back.

What Kind of Time Waster Are You?

You're probably familiar with the personality tests that tell you what kind of parent, employee, or lover you are after you answer a few questions and score the results. Just as different personality styles emerge in these quizzes, there are also a number of styles that people fall into based on how well—or how poorly—they spend their time and organize their lives. Here are a few:

The Rabbit

If you are chronically late, despite setting your watch and alarm clock ahead fifteen minutes, then you take after the March Hare in *Alice's Adventures*

F.Y.I.

It's no surprise why you feel out of control and overwhelmed by the onslaught of information that is competing for your attention on a daily basis. A typical issue of the weekday edition of the *New York Times* has more information in it than an average person who lived in England during the 1600s would encounter in his entire life.

SMART DEFINITION

Wasting time

The real meaning of this term, as you know, tends to be in the eye of the beholder. What others see as wasting time may actually be a refreshing break, an eye in the calm of an impending storm, or a way to transport the brain to sunnier—and happier—climes while the inert body stays behind. The Dave Mathews Band recently sang a hit about the joys of wasting time: eating barbecue, dancing in the street, standing in the rain. However you choose to waste some time, it's important to set aside the time for it, because even if your boss frowns on it, wasting time is often a balm to the soul.

in Wonderland. "I'm late!" is your motto, and you may even have a vanity plate so the world can make no mistake why you're speeding twenty miles an hour over the speed limit: IML8.

The Pack Rat

"But I may need it someday!" is your mantra. If you're a pack rat, you obviously hate to throw anything out. While you may have a clean desk because you cram all the stuff you might need someday into a cardboard box or on a shelf in an already-full closet, just wait until you have to actually find something. This is where pack rats waste a lot of time: trying to put their finger on an obscure document that they don't really need and that should have been tossed out years ago.

The Ostrich

When it comes to the tough stuff, do you tend to stick your head in the sand, hoping that (a) it will disappear eventually, dust to dust and all that jazz, or (b) somebody who's counting on you will finally get disgusted enough and just do it him- or herself. If you're an ostrich, you waste time when you have to spend hours cleaning up the mess that inevitably grows larger the longer your head remains in the sand.

The Dog

"I'll do it! I can do it! Let me do it!" In the time-wasting animal category, you are an overeager canine if you volunteer for every menial task that comes down the pike, totally heedless of the damage it will cause to your schedule and of the mass of incomplete projects and bad tempers you'll leave in your wake. Whether you frantically wave your hand to gain a few brownie points from your boss or to boost your own self-esteem ("If they give it to me, I must really be something!"), one thing is true: a hyper young puppy will be nobody's best friend in no time at all.

The Snake

If you always keep your eyes peeled on other people, where they are and what they're doing instead of on where you've been and what you're accomplishing, then you're a snake. Because the snake can't see its own tail, it's an inveterate time waster but a great scorekeeper. It's great at telling other people how to manage their time better, but doesn't have a clue about the need to do this for itself. Certainly, a snake covers a lot of ground, and frequently takes its time—a rarity in the animal kingdom of time wasters—but without an eye towards its own projects and history, it's destined to spend its life doing nothing more important than digesting rodents.

It's true that there are certain occasions when employing one of these time-wasting animals can work to your advantage, but only in small doses, not as your modus operandi. Once you begin to tune in to how you use and abuse the time in your life, you'll begin to develop a time-savvy instinct about which kind of animal works best in each of your own situations.

Why Should You Want to Manage Your Time Better?

Everyone has his or her own reasons for wanting a better organized life and managed time. However, before you decide exactly how you're going to overhaul your life, you need to evaluate why you want to change. If you do it for the wrong reasons—to please a boss or family member—chances are good that you won't get the full benefit, or that you'll bail out partway through, because something besides your own desire is fueling it.

It's a good idea to get a notebook so you can start working on your time-management program in detail. Even though you may already have a good idea of why you want to manage your time better, answering the following questions will help you to focus on your true motivations. Answer as honestly as you can the questions that appear here and in subsequent chapters, going into as much detail as you need. And be sure to keep your answers in mind as you read through the following chapters.

Self-Assessment
Time-Management Quiz

Assessing your situation and your life is the first step to developing a realistic, sure-to-be-successful time-management program. The following questions will allow you to evaluate where you are now and what it is you are trying to accomplish. Remember to answer honestly.

1. Why do you want to manage your time better? Write down five answers and rank them in order of importance.

2. How much time do you think you'll need?

3. What do you want your life to look like once all the changes you want are integrated into your daily life?

4. What do you like about your mismanaged schedule now?

5. What do you dislike about your mismanaged schedule now?

6. What is the primary benefit you want to gain from learning to manage your time?

7. What's your biggest excuse for not starting to manage your time better?

8. What's one thing you could do right now to change the way in which you manage your time or your schedule?

9. What's do you feel is the biggest thing holding you back from managing your time better? Name one way you could change your schedule to make this obstacle disappear.

10. If you had one extra hour each day to spend in whatever way you wish, how would you choose to spend it?

The Big Picture: The Forest *and* the Trees

Despite the fact that you're unhappy with not having enough time while having too many choices, the truth is that you probably pick at least some of the projects and activities that help to overwhelm your schedule because, simply, they're *fun*. Also, it's quite seductive to keep pushing your own personal limits, to see how much you can handle by yourself before something finally starts to give.

And when things start to give, you probably still don't recognize that you're on perpetual overload. Maybe you'll just get up an hour earlier, or maybe you'll plan an activity five nights a week instead of the three you currently have . . .

And maybe you'll just have a nervous breakdown. In addition to being a speeded-up society, we are also an insatiably curious society, and want to learn as many new things as possible. If you happen to be a recent college graduate, the freedom to pick what you want to learn about is still a heady rush, especially if you were barely able to survive the mind-numbing classes that were necessary for you to earn your degree so you could get a job in a field you expected to love, but where the thrill may have quickly worn off. Obviously this may be the reason you're wasting time on the job, since you're living for your evenings and weekends when you can do what you really want to do, or continuing to muddle through the weeks and months, knowing that there's something you'd like, but you're just not sure what. After all, people who are unhappy with their current lives are more likely to waste time than people who are mostly content.

But there's not enough time for you to do everything you want to do, and so you *have* to continue at your current breakneck speed so you can someday live the life you want to live, right?

Not exactly. Learning how to manage your time effectively means that you'll be better able to get everything done on your various to-do lists, both today's and the list for the rest of your life. This means that you'll have to break out of the mind set that characterizes you as *either* a detail person—one who focuses on the "trees"—*or* an overview person—one who views only the "forest." Both have their advantages and disadvantages when it comes to time management: Tree people know that they accomplish a lot in a certain period of time by focusing on the small things, but they can sometimes have *too* much focus and spend more time on a project than is necessary. Forest people, on the other hand, are great at keeping track of the flow of a project, especially when a number of people are working together on a team, but can sometimes underestimate the importance of the details, resulting in an inferior outcome and perhaps even the need to spend *extra* time redoing a project to get it right.

You'll feel as though you're more in control of your daily schedule—and your life—if you integrate a little of both into your life, the forest *and* the trees. No matter which category you fall into, the exercises and hints in the rest of the book will help you to become more centered, keeping the details and the overall view in the same sight line.

You're probably a little nervous about letting go of your old way of doing things—after all, your old ways haven't been *all* bad, since they've gotten you to where you are today—but with a little effort and attention, along with the desire to create

WHAT MATTERS, WHAT DOESN'T

What Matters
• Evaluating the reasons why you always feel pressed for time.

• Completing a task to your own satisfaction, but not to the point of perfectionism so that it takes time away from other duties.

• Recognizing the primary time-waster style in yourself and in others.

What Doesn't
• Blaming other people and events for your lack of time.

• Rushing through your tasks so you can move on to the next one.

• Badmouthing another person because in your opinion he or she wastes time, or does things in a different manner than you .

more time in your life, you can finally get off the treadmill.

You've learned a little bit about the primary ways in which you tend to waste time, and why you and millions of others are in the same boat. Obviously, this information is useful to know, but if you don't take action you'll continue on the same inefficient track that led you to this book in the first place.

Now's the time to start taking action. Start slowly with some of the suggestions in chapter 2 and the ones that follow; after all, your body and mind have had a lifetime to adjust to your current model of time mismanagement.

THE BOTTOM LINE

Most people feel they don't have enough time to do the things they want to, as well as the things they should. Gaining some insight into the whys behind your particular style of time mismanagement is a great way to get started on the road to feeling you are in control of your life. Once you've identified your problem areas, you can begin to make realistic plans for the dreams that will be possible when you free up your time.

....

Setting Your Priorities

As you know, it's all too easy to get swept away in the undertow of people, activities, and events that make up every day of your life. It can also be very frustrating. You'll have a great head start toward managing your time if you begin to determine which people and tasks need your attention first.

If you're not convinced that it's possible for you to get a firm grip on controlling the way you spend your time—which is infinitely better than having time control you—just keep reading. Even if you take just a tiny step toward determining one of your priorities—and remembering to stick to it—this can be all it takes to help you see how effective time management can drastically affect your daily life, not to mention your blood pressure and stress levels.

Is This an Emergency?

Even though all tasks and activities enter your brain with the same five senses, they usually deserve different levels of consideration and attention, depending on where they fall in your time line. Some need to be taken care of immediately, while others can wait.

Sounds simple, right? Sure, you may be nodding your head, but then why do you have so much trouble determining if a given task needs to be done immediately, or if it can wait? Many people who manage their time poorly assign the same urgency to every task, visitor, and interruption, which often results in missed deadlines or anxious and impatient colleagues. Part of this conditioning, of course, is a result of the egalitarian way in which subjects were presented in school, as though science and English class bore the same weight as gym class, at least in the eyes of your teachers. And of course, ego enters into it as well: after all, you must be good if people start to regard you as the only one competent enough to handle the countless fires they need to have extinguished over the course of the day.

The problem is that you can be *too* good at it, so that you spend most of your day putting out fires that others have started and have no time left to work on your own.

Figuring out whether a task needs immediate action or can wait may be the most valuable time-management technique you can learn. It can also be the most difficult to absorb, since you will have to train yourself to grade every new task before you dig in—or toss it onto your I'll-get-to-it pile—but once you master it, you're halfway there.

Think back to one particularly harried morning—at work or at home—when it seemed as if you were running around in circles, giving one task your attention for only a few minutes before the next demanded your energy, which forced you to abandon the previous task, perhaps leaving it undone the entire day. Jot down a few notes about four or five of the tasks you flitted between that morning and rate each one on a scale of one to five: give it a one if a catastrophic event would have occurred if you didn't finish it, and a five if it didn't matter if it got done that morning or next month.

Now, arrange each task in the order of importance, while also estimating the length of time it would take to complete that task. If you started with the most important task, finished it, and then proceeded to the next one—without interruptions—how many would you have finished? Keep in mind that each task may actually be a small part of a larger project; you should think only of those tasks that needed your attention on that particular morning.

Now think about what you would look like and how you would act while working on these tasks in both your old and new styles: Would you be calm, cool, collected, and less likely to make a mistake, or would you feel frantic and overwhelmed, unsure if you'd be able to check any of your tasks off your list, let alone all of the ones you've scheduled for that morning?

The key to determining the importance of any given task is to first take a deep breath and briefly assess its stature and assign it a priority. An A task means it requires your immediate attention, while a C task can wait and doesn't need much in the way of concentration. Can it wait? Or does it need to get done today? Yes, a frequently used catch phrase in our society is, "I need it yesterday," but since you're learning how to effectively manage your time, yesterday doesn't count.

Some other questions to ask: Where does the task fit into the context of the project, your schedule, as well as the entire picture? If you postpone the task, will the extra time that elapses affect the cost, completion date, or quality of the project? Will it negatively affect another person's schedule? And so on. Just remember to always breathe first, ask yourself a few questions, and then react.

Delegating Tasks; or, No One Is Indispensable

Of course you've heard that two heads are better than one, but in this world, unfortunately, delegation is not a skill that's widely taught either in the schools or on the job. Part of the reason comes down to ego: "If I ask someone else to do it, it looks like I'm slacking off." Another reason is that many of us just don't like to ask a favor of another person: you may wonder how and when you'll have to return the favor, you may feel uncomfortable asking for help, or you've probably been brainwashed into believing that you can handle anything that comes down the pike.

Well, guess what? It's not a sign of weakness to ask for help when you need it. You may even be able to help other people discover their own talents while you reduce your own workload. Whether you are the boss or the employee, the parent or the child, it's normal to need to ask for help at one time or another, either from a higher-up or from someone on a lower rung of the ladder.

If you think the other person won't be able to do the task the way you can, get over it. Though it's probably true that no one will be able to do it quite the way you can, if you start by delegating tasks where either a slightly or radically different work style will not affect the final product, then you'll be freed up to work on and influence more of the areas where a unique style does matter.

Here's one more way to get at the heart of the matter: if you start to regularly parcel out tasks

One of the best ways to delegate work to others is to announce the project and the deadline in a matter-of-fact tone so that others will assume that it's inflexible. Then, if they run into roadblocks in accomplishing the task, it's up to them to meet the deadline.

Kathy Meyer-Poppe, a successful director at Revlon, used this technique with her own staff. "They knew it was truly important when I said, 'I need this by next Friday,' and that I'm not just blowing in the wind," she said. But the other side of the equation is that she left herself open to negotiation when her staff would tell her they were unable to meet the deadline. This kind of reverse negotiation works well when both sides are honest and keep the lines of communication open.

you need completed, you'll be able to take on even more projects! (I knew that would appeal to your basest instincts.)

Now that you're convinced, it's time to start parceling out your workload. And understand that this will take some time.

To ease you into this strange and foreign land, first choose a task that you feel comfortable delegating to someone else. Next, select a person you know will understand clear direction and who you feel will do it to your specifications. Offer help and assistance when necessary, but make it clear to the delegatee that it's up to him to figure things out on his own when it comes to the small questions. Then, when the task is done, offer additional guidance and feedback if necessary, but most of all, give a great big thank you. This will make both of you feel good, and you will be more likely to delegate again in the near future.

It's important to understand that the person to whom you choose to delegate will not necessarily be a coworker or family member, but instead he or she may be an individual or business that specializes in taking the weight—and extra work—off people's shoulders. In fact, outsourcing your menial chores at home and at work to people who are glad to take them off your hands may be the best way to see how delegating can result in a more smoothly run life, leaving you more time to do the good stuff.

After all, if you've ever hired a person to clean your house, even one time, you know how good it feels to let go of some unpleasant chores in your life.

Learning How to Say No

Do you just hate to say no, regardless of the reason? Well, you're not alone. From childhood, we are taught that good children are polite and never say no. Later on, in adulthood, we learn that there are many different shades of no, while there are many reasons for saying yes even when we want to decline.

Possibly the most important reason why you feel you are not in control of how you spend your time is that you underuse this little word. You have probably convinced yourself that you need to say yes when you really want to say no because you fear that if you say no you'll be passed over for promotion, your best friend won't call anymore, your spouse will love you less, your dog will treat you differently, or all of the above. Of course, these fears are all based on your perceptions, which do have a kernel of truth to them. However, whenever you agree to do something that someone asks you to do, what it boils down to is that you have that much less time to spend on accomplishing the tasks that you want and need to get done.

Think about it: it's a hard lesson to learn, but realizing that you're sacrificing your own personal time and challenges because you are emotionally unable to say no is perhaps the best wake-up call you could get. You should also realize that your worst fears of how another person will react when you say no are probably miles away from the reality.

Here's one example: I had invited my sister and her kids up for a few days. Since I don't have kids, I wasn't sure how to act around them. The

TV rarely goes on at our house, but I knew it was constantly on back home at theirs. An hour after they arrived, they asked if they could watch TV, conveniently ignoring the large backyard and the pool they could play in.

My worst fear was that they would throw a temper tantrum. I paused, stammering a bit, then simply said, "No, not right now."

Their reaction? They shrugged, said "Okay," and went outside to play.

Wow, that was it? What was I afraid of?

Ask yourself the same question: What's the worst that could popssibly happen if you say no? And why do you think the other person will react in that fashion?

Think back—you may have to go back a bit—to a specific time when you said no to someone, and I'm not talking about turning down dessert. How did they react? More important, how did you feel when you realized that you could take control of a situation by saying no? I'll bet you felt pretty good and in control.

"Well, maybe I'll just say maybe instead," you may be thinking. After all, after a lifetime of saying yes to just about everyone and everything that has crossed your path, maybe is a sign of progress, right?

Don't do it; the people who have been hearing you say yes for years will hear you utter maybe and think you still mean yes. And then you'll be no better off than before, since saying maybe is a not-so-well-couched way to avoid making any decision at all. If you say it enough times, people may come to view you as wishy-washy.

This doesn't mean that you have to be nasty when you say no. Instead, think about what you'll have to give up if you don't say no. You may also be surprised to discover that usually all that's needed to settle even a complicated issue is a simple no, without the lengthy and overly detailed explanation you feel compelled to offer. Of course, this will take practice, but you are probably well aware of the fact that some of the people you've been saying yes to all these years may have taken advantage of you, asking you to do something distasteful because they already knew what your answer would be.

If this doesn't light a fire under you to learn to say no like a person who values her time and means it, nothing will!

Three Things at Once and One Thing at a Time

Most people have at least a few projects—whether they're work-related or personal—competing for their attention and hours at the same time. Some people tackle them by chipping away a little at each one at the same time, while others work on one project until it's done before going on to the next. When it comes to the wisdom of doing one thing at a time versus stacking several different tasks together, there are two schools of thought about which is more efficient.

People who favor doing one thing at a time believe that completing one task before moving on to the next results in focused bursts of activity that enable you to get more done in less time than if you were hopping around from one job to the

F.Y.I.

It's easier to assert yourself in uncomfortable situations if you are armed with the information you need. First research what it is you're negotiating. Once you are sufficiently informed, you can feel more confident in holding your position or saying no.

A little knowledge is a wonderful way to prepare yourself when it comes to choosing to say yes or no.

next. The opposing group believes that if you are able to juggle several tasks at the same time—like driving to work, talking on the cell phone, and putting on your makeup—you'll still finish them in the same amount of time, and moreover will do so without becoming as bored or stale as you might if you were to concentrate on just one.

The truth is that both approaches can result in increased efficiency, but only in certain cases and only if you don't overdo it. Obviously the juggler applying eye makeup in the car—or on the train, for that matter—is a good candidate for a serious accident, but it's possible to employ both styles and still be able to get your work done in less time than you do now.

The secret is planning ahead. (Is this phrase beginning to sound like a broken record? Good.) If you know you need a large, uninterrupted block of time for a project that requires your full attention, then pull out all the stops—and the phone, fax, and e-mail, if necessary—so that you can get the time you need. It's a good bet that if you tackle it in this focused way, you'll complete the project sooner, and it will be of higher quality than if you were to spread it out over a period of time when you are distracted by several other projects as well.

However, the multitasking approach is a must when several simultaneous deadlines loom before you. Obviously, as you've already discovered, delegating may be the best way out of a tight fix, but lacking that, the best solution is to isolate yourself from as many distractions as possible, and then concentrate on the tasks at hand. In fact, working on several tasks at the same time can actually spark your brain into seeking answers that may not come up if you don't put one project aside temporarily while you work on another. For instance, many people who exercise report that their best ideas and solutions come when they're running or biking, when they've stopped looking directly at a topic or problem and tucked it away just under the realm of consciousness and gone on to do something else as a break.

But you should be careful not to take the idea of multitasking to extremes. Of course, there are those among us who get really bored with only one thing to handle; we tend to thrive on the constant challenge of having another ball thrown at us out of nowhere that we now have to keep airborne. But you may feel compelled to work on more than one project at once because you feel you are being judged: by bosses, families, and coworkers who think you're doing nothing if you're doing just one thing. This could have something to do with our Puritan roots and the belief that "the Devil finds work for idle hands." What others may think, however, is less important than learning about your own limits, and then sticking to them. If you thrive on being a juggler, your biggest temptation may be to say yes to taking on one more project because it means doing just four things at once instead of three, and after all, what's one more? Let this serve as a warning: This innocent query—What's one more?—is the reason some people end up in a house filled with twenty-two cats and little else, when they started out with just two.

SMART DEFINITION

Multitasking

This is one of those ubiquitous terms that originated in the computer industry and was quickly adopted by people in other fields.

Multitasking is used to describe the concurrent running of several programs by a computer system or network. When applied to humans, it means that one person is working on at least two, and usually more, projects at the same time.

It Doesn't Have to Be Perfect

Ah, perfectionism. If you're the type of person who feels that any project you've completed could have been improved in some way, you're not necessarily a perfectionist. If, however, you go back and tinker with a project long after it's been put to bed, when further improvement is a moot point, then you are definitely a perfectionist. Making sure things are perfect is one of the more common techniques to thwart effective time management, since, after all, *nothing* will ever be perfect; even the *Mona Lisa* could be improved.

If you're a perfectionist, you suffer from a double-edged problem: you rarely delegate work to others because you think that other people's work won't meet your own high standards. However, by shouldering all of the responsibility, you're building yourself a house of cards that's impossible to maintain and will eventually collapse, probably much sooner than later, because in addition to taking responsibility for everything around you, you require your work to meet an impossibly high standard that probably matters only to you.

If you recognize that you're a perfectionist, ask yourself these questions:

• Who am I trying to please?

• When my boss and colleagues compliment me on my work, is there a part of me that doesn't believe them?

• What's the worst that will happen if a project doesn't quite meet my exacting standards? More importantly, will anyone notice?

Frequently, people who need to have everything perfect and *still* aren't satisfied with the way things turn out tend to put a lot of weight on what others think about them. The truth is that a perfectionist is frequently heeding an inner voice as he or she strives for an unattainable goal. This voice probably developed during childhood, when a parent, teacher, or another adult did one of two things: they praised him or her for a job well done, or criticized him or her for getting one little thing wrong in a project that was otherwise well done.

Remember, we're our own harshest critics. What happens when your friend confesses that she's embarrassed by the way her hair is sticking up, or that she gained five pounds and is certain that everyone around her has noticed? You probably didn't even notice, even when she brought it up, right?

As a recovering perfectionist, try to apply the same logic to your own life when you notice that something in your surroundings is out of place or otherwise not perfect to your eye. If you mention your discomfort to a friend, and she tells you she didn't even notice, believe her. Chances are she isn't doing it to be nice.

Another reason why people are perfectionists is that they fear change. After all, if you're able to stay with the tried-and-true, and tinker with it endlessly, even long after the project was actually completed, you don't have to leave the familiar task behind and begin with a new project, where the rules may be unfamiliar and the newness may make you nervous.

F.Y.I.

People who live in small rural towns that are at least twenty miles from the nearest supermarket quickly realize they need to plan ahead if they don't want to spend half their waking hours in their car.

Many use different variations of what I call batching: One type is to buy the entire week's groceries during one shopping trip. Another is to batch smaller chores—combining a bank deposit with a trip to the hardware store—in the same town. A third way is to really plan ahead and go to the nearest large city once a year for new school clothes, once a month to a warehouse club, and perhaps once every four years to buy a new car.

No wonder Internet shopping has caught on like rapid fire among people who live in small, remote towns.

If you tend toward perfectionism, for whatever reason, the first thing is to figure out if you're the only one who notices when something is not perfect in your eyes. With the next project you take on, take time to envision in your mind's eye the time, skills, and special touches that are required to get the job done. Are any of those special touches superfluous, and do they take time away from the next project on your agenda? As was the case earlier in this chapter when you learned to distinguish between emergencies and those tasks that can wait, you'll need to apply a critical eye toward determining which projects under your care truly do need to be perfect, and which will be just as successful if the minimums are met, without any additional frosting on the cake.

You are your own harshest critic. Certainly, sometimes you need to put your entire concentration into trying to make something perfect: a special presentation, a twenty-fifth anniversary party, or another rare event. But since you are human, mistakes will happen. In fact, mistakes can sometimes actually enhance an occasion, turning what may have started as a stuffy event where people felt uncomfortable—because even people who aren't perfectionists can be intimidated by something that is so obviously beyond their league and scope of accomplishment—into a jovial affair that people will remember for years.

Putting Off Until Tomorrow . . .

Ah, procrastination. You may think that procrastination is the flip side of the coin from perfectionism, but the two can actually go hand in hand, or they can be mutually exclusive. If you're a perfectionist, you may regularly put off taking action on a project because you know that no matter how much time you or someone else spends on it, the final result won't meet your high standards.

On the other side, however, you may be a master at procrastination because you feel overwhelmed and unable to make a decision, so you postpone doing something long enough so that someone else will come along to do it. Either that, or it will fall by the wayside. Procrastination is an insidious trap, and it's easy to fall into. While an occasional bout with procrastination is normal, and even viewed as a welcome break in some instances, under less than optimal conditions—like working with a difficult boss or balancing your checkbook when you know the final figure is going to depress you—it can quickly spread to influence most, if not all, parts of your life.

The major problem that arises if you continually procrastinate is that your productivity will drop, which will make you feel useless and unworthy, which will sap your energy, making your productivity decrease even more. It's hard to break out of this cycle by yourself. In most instances in which you tend to habitually postpone a task, let's face it: it doesn't go away on its own. When you do finally start chipping away at it, when you finally finish, you may look back and think, "That wasn't so bad."

SMART SOURCES

If you're having trouble proceeding with a project because you're letting your procrastination get the best of you, maybe you need a stronger boost.

Inspire yourself by reading *Do It Now!: Break the Procrastination Habit* by Dr. William J. Knaus and John W. Edgerly.

If you prefer to use audiotapes for self-improvement work, one good tape is *Increase Your Energy: Conquering Procrastination* by Robert Griswold.

WHAT MATTERS, WHAT DOESN'T

What Matters

• Assessing each interruption on its own merits to determine how to react.

• Saying no to preserve your own schedule and sanity.

• Postponing a task when you're under deadline for something else.

What Doesn't

• Treating every interruption as a dire emergency.

• Saying maybe when you really need to say no.

• Continually procrastinating on a project when you just don't want to do it.

The best way to break out of an extended cycle of procrastination, whether on the job or working on a project at home, is to follow the advice of a woman who rarely hesitates and is easily frustrated whenever she hears a friend give a lame excuse for why she can't get to a particular task: "Just one-two-three bungee!" As though you're jumping off a cliff, attached only to a stretchy rubber cord, the best thing to do is to stop thinking about the fact that you're not doing something, and let instinct and action take over: plug your nose, close your eyes, and fling yourself over the cliff. This is not the time to allow yourself to get distracted by the thought of checking your e-mail or by all the *what-ifs* that pop into your head. Just plunge in headfirst and do it. Once you've started, you may wonder why you were postponing it for so long. And though one group of people is famous for their particular brand of procrastination—I'm referring here to writers— their reasons are the same: they're thinking too much about doing it and allowing the thought and fear of what they might discover intimidate them. After all, the idea of writing the tens of thousands of words necessary in order to fill a book can be overwhelming. As a result, many people never start.

In any case, whether you're putting off writing a letter or postponing cleaning the basement, in addition to just plunging into the task without thinking about it first, you may find it easier to handle if you initially break the task down into baby steps. For example, you don't have to clean the entire basement by lunchtime; given the fact that the junk down there may have taken years, even decades, to accumulate, you should be realistic about it. Tell yourself that you're going to clean off and organize the junk in one bookcase or dresser. Then when you finish, take a break before you tackle the next section.

A few reformed procrastinators claim that another way to blast through a particularly ugly bout of inertia is to get the toughest job out of the way first. This may not necessarily be the longest one, but a project that you know from experience will require the bulk of the energy and brain-power you'll expend in a day. If you also integrate an earlier suggestion—writing down a list of tasks you need to accomplish that day and rating them in their order of priority—you won't have to think about whether you should start this project or finish off that chore, and end up wasting a lot of time trying to figure out all the angles. Ponder it briefly, then make a decision and write it down. Getting it down on paper can be the most important step you take toward ending your tendency toward procrastination; many people don't believe it's true until it's written down in black and white. Consider the list as flexible in case an unforeseen emergency crops up, but once one task is written down and then completed, move on to the next item on your list. Yes, it sounds easy, but many of the most seemingly difficult tasks you'll face in your life are easy; it's all that thinking and analysis you do that makes them sound more complex than they really are.

If you still get stuck, here are some tried-and-true methods for breaking through the dreaded procrastination:

• Turn off the voice in your head that's leading you to procrastinate and replace it with a famous nonprocrastinating voice of authority, like General George Patton or Colin Powell. Or perhaps use a role model from your childhood, where a kind word would start you off on your path without having to think twice about it.

• Tell somebody what you're going to do and when you're going to start, and then do it. Then make sure to report back to that person to provide an update on your progress.

• If your major obstacle is a messy desk, get everything off of it except the things you need to work on the task at hand. Before you replace the piles of paper, however, read chapter 4 to learn how to organize your desk.

Okay, so you've learned how to differentiate between true emergencies and those tasks that you can put on hold for a bit, and a little about the value of delegation and turning down work when it comes to managing your time. And while you may never totally let go of your perfectionistic and/or procrastinating tendencies, at least you are aware of them and can relax their grip on your life.

Now comes the part where you can actually put these time-management strategies into play where it counts: in your daily schedule.

THE BOTTOM LINE

The first step in time management is to decide which people, places, and activities you want to take precedence in your life. You'll learn how to integrate them into your daily schedule so that you can achieve a balance that works best for you. Another important step is to recognize those habits that are sabotaging your efforts at managing your time, and then work to eliminate them from your life.

CHAPTER 3

....

Planning Your Schedule

• Knowing how you spend—and waste—your time will help you plan the schedule that works best for you.

• Figure out the time of day when you tend to be most alert, and then schedule your most important tasks during those hours.

• To increase the quality and quantity of your work, get into the habit of taking a short break—or even a nap—every few hours.

• Sleeping even one extra hour a night can make you radically more alert and productive during the day.

• When your plans get thrown off track, go with the flow instead of trying to fight a situation that is beyond your control.

• Scheduling rewards into a particularly hectic day will help to balance out all of your hard work.

People who know how to manage their time well usually have one skill mastered: They are aware of where they are in their schedules at all times. They may not be crazy about it, and it may have taken them a long time to train themselves, but they are able to keep their entire day in focus as they progress through each activity. Schedule-savvy people are also pretty clear about the length of time that any given task should take and are careful to end an activity at the scheduled time, within reason.

That is not to say that skilled time managers are obsessive about adhering to their schedule, but they do know that if they cut themselves a little slack on one project and then run a bit long on another, this extra time will snowball and they will end up spending a good deal of their time trying to catch up. Although planning for this much detail and accuracy in your own schedule may sound like an impossible achievement, it is possible for you to learn how to get a better grip on your schedule. You must start by discovering where you tend to fritter away your time.

Where Did the Time Go? Your Daily Time-Waster Schedule

Before you can manipulate your schedule so that it provides a big boost to your efficiency at home and at work, you need to first examine all the ways in which you *don't* make the most effective use of your time. The best way to do this is by keeping a detailed record that spells out exactly how you spend every minute of every day—or at least in five-minute increments.

From the time you get up in the morning until the time you turn out the light at night, start to write down every single activity, so that every minute is accounted for. Once you see everything down in writing, you'll be able to get an accurate picture of where your time goes, and where you need to make corrections, from the half hour you spent surfing the Internet when you should have been writing that report to the extra five minutes you spent chatting with the waitress at your favorite lunch place to the twenty minutes in the evening when you read your son a story before he went to sleep. Write it all down!

To start, try to keep track of at least two days during the week and at least one weekend day. It's a good idea to perform this exercise on a day when you haven't scheduled anything out of the ordinary. Write down the time you start an activity, and the time you proceed to the next, whether or not you've completed the previous task. In the second column, describe the activity as specifically as you can. Then place that activity into its particular category: eating, driving, cleaning, playing with the kids, reading, or any other category that is relevant to your lifestyle. Then note whether the activity was work-related, personal, or for school, church, or a community event. Some may fall into more than one category.

You'll need to be sure to include any interruptions, like a coworker stopping by to chat for fifteen minutes in the morning, as well as any phone calls. In the next column, write the amount of time spent on that activity, rounded off to the nearest five minutes. In fact, you may want to

F.Y.I.

Do you think that five minutes here and ten minutes there don't add up to a whole hill of beans? It's entirely possible to lose an eye-opening amount of time by wasting a few minutes several times a day. But there are some things you can actually do and check off your list that take only a few minutes of your time:

• Return a phone call.

• Scan through today's newspaper.

• Plan and write down your to-do list for tomorrow.

• Put away that basket of folded laundry that's been sitting in the hall for several days.

• Write a thank-you note to a friend.

record your schedule in a spreadsheet program so that you can manipulate the numbers in order to see how adding ten minutes to one activity or shaving fifteen minutes off another will affect your overall schedule. Below is an example of a time-tracker that you can use.

You may be tempted to alter your activities or to clean up the data so that you look more effective in spending your time than you really are, but that will skew the results and prevent you from making

Monday

Time	Activity	Category	Work, Play or Other	Amount of Time
7:45 – 8:10 A.M.	Drove to work	Driving	Work	25 minutes
8:10 – 8:30	Read mail	Reading	Work	20 minutes
8:30 – 8:45	Chatted with boss	Meeting	Work	15 minutes
8:45 – 9:05	Phone calls to daughter's teacher	Conference	Home	20 minutes
9:05 – 10:30	Worked on report	Writing	Work	85 minutes
10:30 – 11:20	Staff meeting	Meeting	Work	50 minutes
11:20 – 11:35	Drove to lunch	Driving	Work	15 minutes
11:35 – 12:55 P.M.	Lunch	Eating, business	Work	85 minutes

your new and improved schedule the best it can be. Instead, try to go about the day in your usual manner; the only difference is that you're writing it all down, and including every little detail.

Add up the amount of time you've spent each day performing a particular task. For example, if you regularly spend thirty minutes to drive back and forth to work, and then another hour driving your kids around to their afterschool activities, that's ninety minutes of driving per day. You're awake for almost seventeen hours each day, or 1,020 minutes; that means you spend almost 10 percent of the time that you're awake driving in the car. As you add up the figures, calculate the totals as a percentage of your waking hours. Some of the numbers may surprise you.

As you look over the figures, try to envision where you could cut some time, and where you would like to add more. Daydream about what the possibility of having some extra time—especially more personal time—would do to your overall outlook. And then hold that thought.

When Do You Work Best?

When it comes to scheduling the best time to do a particular task, if you have any say in the matter, your own energy level and cycle of alertness should affect your decision. After all, what good is it if you schedule two free hours at the end of your workday for reading, writing, painting, or pursuing another favorite hobby if it's difficult for you to keep your eyes open at that time of day?

F.Y.I.

Here are a few eye-opening statistics about the average person's time:

• A total of 16 years will be spent working.

• An additional 15 years of life are spent sleeping.

• Any task that takes 30 minutes each day will take up a total of one week's time for every year of the person's life.

Similarly at work, if an important project comes up that requires you to spend all of your afternoons for the next two weeks working on it you'll find it next to impossible to do a good job if you tend to concentrate best in the morning and your boss insists that you have to cover a colleague's phone during the mornings over those two weeks.

You've undoubtedly heard about larks and owls: some people work best in the morning while others take longer to get up to speed and do their best work in the afternoons or evenings.

No matter which category you fall into—or even if you're somewhere in the middle, or your energy cycle has a tendency to shift occasionally—here's one rule you should follow: you should perform low-priority tasks, or even grunt work, during the hours when you're not operating at your absolute peak. This way, you can save your most important tasks and projects for the times when you're operating at the top of your mental capacity. For instance, if you're a lark, try to set aside the morning for those tasks that are particularly challenging or that require your full concentration. Then you can use the afternoon for low-energy activities, like answering phone calls, reading, or catching up on correspondence. Owls should do the same, only at the opposite times.

Regardless of whether you're an owl or a lark, one way to enhance your effectiveness is to arrange your schedule so that the last couple of items you check off your list at the end of the day are relatively quick and simple to accomplish. Why? Finishing up your day with a few tasks that are no-brainers sets a positive tone to the end of your day so you leave feeling successful, making you more likely to return the next morning in the same mood. In addition, some people find that it's difficult to start the next morning by focusing on a task that ended on a note of frustration the previous day. If you are able to complete those additional tasks, leaving fewer loose ends to tie up the next day, you're more likely to begin working in a positive frame of mind, which more often than not will set the tone and pace of your entire day.

However, sometimes a particular project will carry you through the down phase of your energy cycle if it's exciting enough. For example, if you are working on a project that you find fascinating, even though the time you've blocked out to work on it occurs during one of your low-energy periods, you may find that the time of day doesn't matter at all. Sure, it may take a little time for you to get up to speed, but a project that's thoroughly engrossing can make you forget that you haven't had that second cup of coffee—and more important, you may find that you don't even need it.

In any case, if your energy starts to fade, you may keep going until you get your second wind, but a better idea—and a way to almost guarantee that you *have* a second wind—is to take a short break. You'll find out next how to integrate regular breaks into your day and how they can improve your overall productivity.

F.Y.I.

Whether you're an owl or a lark, you should know that during the down part of your cycle, you're only working at 50 percent or less than your peak operating capacity. This is why it's so important to schedule the tasks that require your full brainpower for the times of day when you're up for it.

Taking a Break

In this workaholic society of ours where many people think they have to go all out at work and play lest it seem like they're slacking off, the concept of taking a break—whether it's a fifteen-minute time out after a three-hour stretch of uninterrupted work or a much-needed five-day vacation after fin-

Some people find that the best way to motivate themselves to take a break is to inject a little pampering into their time out. One woman closes the door to her office, turns on the radio to a classical station, and touches up her manicure. A top executive who suffers from chronic neck pain uses his break as an opportunity to lie down on his back on the floor and cradle his neck with a special orthopedic pillow with built-in acupressure points. He closes his eyes and lets the machine work its magic for around fifteen minutes, and then he's ready to begin work again.

ishing a project that lasted for several months—is seriously underrated. In fact, the well-kept secret is that regularly scheduled breaks can actually make managing your time a breeze, and you can also become more effective and productive in everything you do.

The first thing to realize is that taking a break and being interrupted are not the same thing. They may have a few things in common, in turning your attention away from whatever you're concentrating on, but they're on opposite ends of the control spectrum: one, the break, is initiated by you and therefore the timing occurs when you most need it, while an interruption always occurs on someone else's schedule, and may come right when you're operating at your peak of productivity.

You know that when you're concentrating on a particular task for any extended period of time, after a while—it could be one hour, maybe three—your attention starts to fade and your thinking turns mushy. A half hour ago you were chugging along, oblivious to everything and everyone around you, totally focused on the task at hand. Now, suddenly, you find yourself starting to slow down a bit; you search for a word that just doesn't come, you read the same paragraph over and over, or you start to think about lunch.

At this point, many people figure that if they just keep going and push on through, their concentration will return and they'll be able to get more done than if they took a break to get some air or have a snack. However, this usually doesn't pan out; those who continue to work through a dip in their energy and concentration levels usually find the quality of their output is about half or less of what it was at the peak of their cycle. What frequently happens is that they end up having to go back later to redo their work, or else accomplish only half the quantity of work they were capable of when they were fresh.

The person who took a break, however, switched his focus away from his work, had a snack, maybe read part of a mystery novel. When he returns to his work a half hour or so later, he's refreshed and able to pick up where he left off, producing the same quantity and quality of work that he did before he stopped. He won't have to spend extra time redoing the kind of inferior output that results from poor concentration and foggy thinking—and he may have had new insight into a thorny problem he was grappling with.

Undoubtedly you've experienced times when you looked too closely at a problem, your eyes started to cross, and solutions were slow to come. But when you took a break and switched the focus of your conscious mind to something else, your unconscious mind was able to get some significant work done. The greatest ideas frequently come when we're not thinking directly about a problem. As with a game of darts or during target practice on a shooting range, in order to hit the bull's-eye, you sometimes have to look away from the center.

That's what taking breaks will accomplish. Of course, taking a nap for a break can be even better, especially if you woke up tired and haven't felt better as the day continued. The trick is to limit a nap to no more than twenty or thirty minutes for maximum effectiveness. Any more than that, and you start to fall into REM sleep, the deepest kind of sleep that you can experience. Once that happens, you are unlikely to wake up feeling refreshed. Whether you wake up naturally or from having your nap interrupted by someone else, you'll probably feel groggy and disoriented.

SMART SOURCES

Besides back pain, sleep deprivation is one of the most common complaints among American adults today. If you suffer from a particularly stubborn case of insomnia, you might check into a sleep lab at a nearby university to discover the reasons for your chronic lack of sleep. You can find a list of them online at www.sleepnet.com

Other book and mail-order resources include the following:

50 Ways to Sleep Better by Neil B. Kavey
Sleep-Net Corporation
www.sleepnet.com

Sleep

If taking a break is the high school version of managing your time, then sleep—and learning how to do more of it and how to use it to help you to work more effectively and efficiently—is the doctoral thesis.

It's no surprise that most people in North America are sleep-deprived. With all the things that compete for our attention, and our lengthy to-do lists both at home and at the office, sleep is often one of the first activities to get cut. If this is your method of grabbing extra hours, though it may seem like the only possible alternative at the time, remember, you're only robbing Peter to pay Paul, and you'll eventually pay for your sleep imbalance. It won't necessarily occur the next day, but the cumulative effect of going weeks, even months, on end with insufficient sleep can result in a dramatic drop in your productivity level. You may have been able to get away with it when you were in your twenties, but it gets harder as you get older. And when you're habitually getting less sleep than you need, it may even be dangerous to go to work as usual if you're operating heavy equipment or if other people are placing their trust in you.

One unique phenomenon that can occur if you are extremely sleep-deprived is called microsleep, a phase where you fall asleep for only a few seconds, usually without closing your eyes. This is the body's way of compensating for its sleep deficit: it will grab some shut-eye whenever it can get it. One of the most common situations in which microsleep happens is also the scariest: driving a car at night. You know the feeling: you're tired, it's late, it's dark, and although you're driving, the movement and hum of the car just lulls you to sleep for a few seconds. But that's all it takes. The majority of truck accidents occur when the driver falls into microsleep, since truck drivers are notorious for driving long hours without taking a break for even a nap. The result, of course, is that they don't get enough sleep.

The only surefire cure for microsleep, whether you're a truck driver or a secretary, is to get more sleep at night. And adding as little as an hour of sleep each night can make a huge difference in your productivity and alertness during the day. Think about it: if you spend just one extra hour sleeping at night, the next day, instead of just dragging yourself through your day, accomplishing perhaps three hours of work (if you're lucky), you will be far more alert and able to operate at peak levels for six or more hours. Think of it as the equivalent of tripling your money.

Fortunately, of all the suggestions you'll read about in the *Smart Guide to Managing Your Time* getting more sleep is one of the easiest things you can do—of course, that is, if you don't worry about all the things that are going undone because you're going to bed one hour earlier. Just trust in the process: you'll be able to get more work done during the day if you take a little extra time to sleep at night.

If you find that you're so used to walking around sleep-deprived that it's difficult for you to fall asleep at night, here are a few things to try:

• Be sure to get enough exercise during the day. Even a brisk ten-minute walk during your lunch hour will help.

• Use your bed only for sleeping and intimacies, not for eating, talking on the phone, or watching

SMART DEFINITION

Microsleep

Microsleep is a condition that occurs when you're suffering from sleep deprivation. Basically, you fall asleep for just a few seconds, often without even closing your eyes. Others may perceive that you've lost your focus and attention for several seconds. Periods of microsleep are mostly likely to occur before dawn and during the middle of the afternoon. Microsleep is usually distinguished by a blank stare or the snapping of the head as you suddenly awaken.

SMART MONEY

Azriela Jaffe, mother, consultant, and author of *Honey, I Want to Start My Own Business: A Planning Guide for Couples* and several other small-business self-help books, accomplishes what some people have referred to as "an impossible amount." She attributes part of her success to her ability to go with the flow.

"When I start my day, I think about what I want to accomplish in my work and family responsibilities for the entire day and maximize my ability to do two things at once, but I also let things slide," she says. "For example, I don't worry about only making dinner at dinnertime, but do it when I can steal a few minutes. My six-month-old won't let me work, so I'll put together a stew with one hand."

TV. You can trick your body into a Pavlovian response by convincing it that the bed means sleep.

• Don't drink coffee, tea, or other beverages with caffein within four hours of bedtime.

• Make sure your bedroom is as well ventilated as possible; a stuffy room often results in poor sleep.

Going with the Flow

You can plan your schedule down to the last possible detail, building in time for breaks and even some open-ended time, but often when push comes to shove, even the best-laid plans and schedules get thrown off course. In fact, if your life doesn't include a fair number of emergencies and unexpected wrenches tossed into the works, perhaps you should check your pulse.

The first thing to be aware of as you're drawing up your schedule for the next day, week, or month, is that when you reach the end of that time period, what you actually did and how you lived will look much different from what you expected. Of course, it would be nice if you could schedule a certain period each day to deal with emergencies—say, for example, Thursday 3:00 to 4:00 P.M.: Emergency Time—but unfortunately life is not that predictable.

You probably know that it doesn't help when you get bent out of shape over an unexpected interruption—like a sick child or a disabled car—and that it may even make things worse, since the worry and stress that develop may distract you or delay future work. But you can do several things to deal with an unforeseen interruption, and perhaps lessen its impact on the rest of your schedule as well as your sanity.

First, consider whether it's feasible to implement any of the time-management strategies you have learned so far, or that you discover later, after you finish reading the *Smart Guide to Managing Your Time.* For instance, if it's impossible for you to deal with the matter at hand immediately, can you delegate someone else to take care of it for you? Say your car has broken down in your driveway, for example, and you had to catch a ride into work with your neighbor. Instead of taking the next morning off to sit at home and wait for your mechanic or service center to tow the car, with you following behind, and then sitting in the waiting room for a couple of hours waiting for the diagnosis, you can give the garage directions to your house and have them call you at work with their recommendations. Or you can hire an errand service or neighborhood concierge business to take care of the problem for you. In fact, after you see how smoothly things run when you hire someone else to take care of a problem in an emergency, you should seriously consider hiring the same company or person to perform some or all of the everyday mundane tasks that you do not have time for as well.

In fact, emergency situations frequently offer you the first chance to implement many of the time-management skills you are reading about. Why? One reason is that retraining yourself takes time, and if you had any extra time, why would you be reading a book that tells you how to manage it better? But a more likely reason is that you'll tuck many of the ideas away for future use, because it's impossible to implement them all at once; some are necessarily case-sensitive.

SMART DEFINITION

Pareto Principle

A common formula known as the Pareto Principle is a variation of the small business 80/20 creed, which holds that 80 percent of a company's revenue comes from only 20 percent of its customers. The Pareto Principle suggests that 80 percent of your activities result in only 20 percent of your outcomes, while 20 percent of your efforts affect a whopping 80 percent of your results. Are you spinning your wheels?

An important thing to keep in mind when it comes to time management is that you also can go too far in the other direction, and try to control your time *too* much. When life doesn't follow your orders, much like a stubborn child, you can do one of two things: you can fight it, or you can learn to manage it. Yes, it will throw your original plans off, but you'll live. The important things to remember are these:

• Expect the unexpected.

• Be prepared to deal with emergencies in whatever form they take.

• After the emergency is over, take a quick survey of how the interruption has affected your regular schedule.

• Employ other time-management strategies to get back on track.

• Sit back and wait for the next emergency to arise.

• Remember to go with the flow!

Building In Rewards

You know what they say about all work and no play, right? Becoming a whiz at managing your time will turn you into a productive and efficient machine, but if work is all you do, then your heavy workload may cause your life to lose its meaning.

Building rewards into your schedule is similar to taking a break when you know you'll need it in order to get a second wind, but it's slightly different: it requires you to deliberately plan an activity into your schedule to reward yourself for all the hard work you have been doing. If you're one of those people who says, "My work *is* my reward," don't turn the page so quickly. Though people who live in North America love to play and participate in leisure time activities, many of us are not as carefree as we look: for one thing, we may be feeling guilty during every second that we're playing. That old Puritan work ethic can be stubborn and can interfere with the pursuit of life, leisure, and happiness.

One of the toughest things that you may have struggled with as an adult is the idea of achieving a sense of balance in your life. Human beings do not thrive on work alone, and there is a fine line between too much work and what we feel—usually not accurately—is too much play. Paradoxically, the idea of rewarding yourself with some play time is particularly crucial during those periods when it seems you're filling your every waking moment with work in order to meet a critical deadline. Predictably, you may feel it's impossible: "How can you sit there and tell me I need to go and play when I've got all this work staring me in the face?"

Well, yes, that is exactly what you need to do. If you don't take a playful break during your workday, your ideas and thinking are likely to go stale. And especially when you're under a crazy deadline with no time to breathe, that is the best time to take a break. It may help if you think of it as part of your work time: consider it a chance to meditate on what you've accomplished so far and what still needs to be done if it helps encourage you to take the time off. By the way, the best way

WHAT MATTERS, WHAT DOESN'T

What Matters
• Staying aware of the most common ways that you tend to waste time.

• Actively fantasizing about all the ways you would spend any extra time.

• Sitting tight to read more about the best ways for you to manage your time better.

What Doesn't
• Getting bent out of shape because you're running five minutes behind your schedule.

• Being totally unrealistic about the amount of free time you'll have because you arrived at work a half hour early.

• Radically altering your life overnight by integrating a number of drastic lifestyle and work style changes into your day.

to do this is to absolutely act like a child: go to the playground and hang upside down on the monkey bars or go to the gym and splash around in the pool, or . . . well, you get the idea.

Here are some other ways you can reward yourself for a job well done as well as building in necessary time-outs:

• When you complete a project, splurge on an item that you would normally regard as a gift for somebody else and not a purchase for yourself; for example, a pound of organic coffee beans or an expensive silk scarf or tie.

• Every time you complete a task in a long-term project, toss a dollar or some coins in a jar. When the project is finished, take the money that's accumulated and buy something that's a total luxury.

• Or, whenever you check another task off your list, leave the office for a half hour. Turn off the computer and the lights, close the door, and leave the premises to browse in a store, go for a walk, or have a cup of coffee and indulge by reading the novel you've been putting off.

You may have suspected that you weren't making the best possible use of your time, but now you've started to learn about the small parts of your schedule that sabotage your sincere efforts to get ahead of the clock. Now that you've begun to get a clearer idea of the various ways in which you spend your time, it's time to call out all of the tools and skills you'll need to start to integrate more efficiency and quality into your schedule every day.

Up next is your big chance to dig right in and

get your hands dirty: you'll start to organize your space. This is the best time-management task to do first because once you have your physical surroundings in some kind of order, you'll be sorely tempted to bring order into the rest of your disorganized life.

THE BOTTOM LINE

You may find that it's difficult to whip your schedule into shape because after all, you can't just tear it up and start over again: you have to work with what you have.

That's why it's important to not only pay attention to the parts of your schedule that you can control, but also to look for—and expect—those you can't. Plus, doing those tasks that initially appear to be counterproductive—like taking a break and getting more sleep—will provide a great surprise when you see how effective they can be as a time management tool.

CHAPTER 4

....

Organizing Your Space

A *clean desk is the sign of a sick mind . . . It looks messy, but at least I know where everything is . . . Well, then, I'll just close the door so you don't have to look at it!*

How many of these excuses have you used to justify your unorganized and plainly messy workspace, whether at home or at work? If you're like many people who clearly need to instill more order into their lives, you might secretly confess that it *would* help if you could find things more easily and quickly, but your first reaction is that you don't have the time. Your second—and most well-hidden—response would be to dig in your heels against anyone who criticizes you and also gives you advice.

As is the case with unlearning any bad habit, the time you spend rearranging your space will be paid back to you many times over. Think about how the next time you reach for a book or important piece of paper, you'll be able to locate it within seconds, instead of the minutes or even hours it takes now. The time you spent to organize your workspace will be worth every second.

The Curse of Horizontal Surfaces

For those people who haven't previously thought about organizing their lives—and in fact secretly revel in their well-earned reputation as a messy-but-creative type—any piece of furniture that offers up a flat area that can hold stacks of papers, folders, books, or anything else, is a great excuse to maintain their particular brand of filing and organization. This means that any shelf, desk, table, chair, or even the floor is a likely candidate to serve as a paper-holding tank when they need to clear a space in order to work but don't have the time to file each item—or, more likely, they don't even have a straightforward system for organizing their papers.

If you're smiling and nodding your head in recognition, you're a longtime member of the club that believes that any horizontal surface is the equivalent of a file folder in a well-organized filing cabinet. "I don't work that way," you might gripe. "Besides, it takes too much time to file away each individual piece of paper, or to walk downstairs and put away a book in its proper place, and it will interfere with my stream-of-consciousness way of thinking, and whatever I'm working on will suffer as a result . . ."

Is this you? You're in good company. In fact, the best creative minds have been guilty of this method of thinking: the excuse that is given most often is that if some semblance of order is imposed on your surroundings, you'll be less likely to think creatively because you'll first have to censor your thoughts with visions of organization.

You know the scenario: whenever people visit your home or office and are immediately confronted with a scene right out of an explosion at a paper factory, they smile and shake their heads knowingly, as if your work environment explains everything about you that they long suspected. And whenever you have to interrupt what you're doing to find something you need, though you hate to admit it, most of the time locating the item is as frustrating as trying to find the perfect word that's on the tip of your tongue: you know it's there, but it's just out of reach. You'd like to

STREET SMARTS

For a New Year's resolution one year, one chronically disorganized woman rid her office of every horizontal surface except one: her desk. And even that she downsized and filled with her computer and telephone so she wouldn't be tempted to lay down a stack of papers that she'd "get around to."

She bought a filing system and office organizer and then spent one long weekend setting up her files, cleaning out her closets, and throwing out most of the stacks of paper that had previously served as her filing system. It was radical, but she knew this marathon weekend overhaul would be life-changing.

change things and get your home and workspace more organized, but feel it's out of character for you, and that it would detract from the spirit in your work if you had to be more disciplined and organized.

The truth of the matter is, however, that your creativity and work ethic will soar even more once you take the time to get organized. Having a place for your papers and important stuff will not only free up time that you can spend on your creative projects, it will free up your physical and mental energy as well—energy you can spend doing the kinds of things you enjoy and find inspiring.

Horizontal surfaces are great when it comes to having something to put your computer on as well as a place to eat your meals and to get your eight hours worth of shut-eye. But when it comes down to organizing your worldly possessions and important documents, vertical surfaces are a much better way to get control of your life and to better manage your time.

The Paper Trap

Remember when the idea of having a "paperless" society or the electronic office first began to infiltrate the nation's science news pages? Around the time that desktop computers began to be promoted for personal use at home, one of the selling points of the machines for both home and office use was that they would cut down on or totally eliminate the unruly piles of paper that you could never seem to get out from under.

Right. Well, we all know what has happened. The exploding popularity of high-tech equipment for the home and small office—personal computers, copiers, fax machines, laser and color printers, and scanners—has resulted in a sheer overload of paper. Even if you have a copy of a document stored on a disk, you more than likely also have a hard copy buried somewhere in that teetering stack of papers that is leaning against the printer and threatening to collapse the next time you walk by it.

In part, the reason why many of us view a horizontal surface as both a saving grace and a curse is that it makes it possible to deal with the onslaught of too much paper in our lives. The tendency to save papers is caused by one aspect of the overly cautious part of our souls: we might need it again. In a world filled with uncertainty and seemingly endless revolving doors in both our professional and personal lives, a stack of papers is at least something we can control, even if it looks like it's out of control. And you don't have to be a pack rat to fall victim to this way of thinking, either. After all, the unruly explosion of paper that permeates your office is not necessarily caused by printing out all the documents you've downloaded from the Internet in the last year. Instead, think about all the reasons why you are holding on to the report you wrote on polar bears when you were in the third grade. And why is it that you can put your finger on it within five seconds while you don't have a clue where to find your birth certificate or passport?

Even though a lot of the excess paper in our lives results from correspondence and lists that we personally generate and produce, the onslaught of catalogs, offers, and other solicitations—requested and unsolicited—that are received in the mail by just one household in the course of a week would be enough to suffocate an elephant. How much of

F.Y.I.

If you subscribe to an Internet mailing list and regularly print out some of the more informative posts to save for future reference, one good way to store them while still having them at your fingertips is to keep them in a looseleaf binder. Organize the notebook into sections with manila paper dividers and tabs. Then, every time you print out a post, use a special hole puncher and put the printout in the appropriate section. Not only will this keep your desk area neat, but your hard drive and your Internet service provider's server will benefit as well, since you don't have to keep the postings in your e-mail file permanently.

this mail do you immediately toss, whether or not you take a look at it first? And then, like the other pieces of paper that you hold on to, how many catalogs and offers do you add to the growing stack, thinking that you'll look at them again next week or next month?

Just to give you a bit of an indication of just how far off the high-tech pundits were when they described their vision of a paperless society, here are some things you should know:

• In just one year, all the businesses and government agencies located in Washington, D.C., use so many reams of plain white bond copy paper that if each sheet was placed end to end, the path would run to and from the moon at least ten times over.

• Since 1990, the consumption of paper in the United States has more than doubled.

• You probably use twice the amount of paper that you think you do.

It will take a combination of awareness and effort to start reducing the amount of paper that floods your life. Keep reading to discover some of the ways that will work best for you.

Clean Off Your Desk!

It should come as no surprise to hear that there is a national holiday known as Clean Off Your Desk Day. The only problem is that the people who could benefit from it the most—and you're included—may have clipped out the notice when they first heard about it, but it quickly got swallowed up in the mass of paper on their desks. And the next time it surfaced was probably three months *after* the holiday, and the only reason it showed up was because the pile it was stuck in—inevitably in the "I'll Get Around to This Someday" pile—tipped over from its own weight.

The more likely excuse for the state of your desk is that you're too busy. You tell your boss—or yourself—that you would like to be able to work at a clean desk, but you just don't have the time.

But wait, you *do* have the time to spend an hour digging through three or four different "I'll Get Around to This Someday" piles for one piece of paper, right? What's wrong with this picture?

It's nothing that a little organization and a few large garbage bags won't solve. As you've already discovered, the learning curve of cleaning and organizing your desk will undoubtedly consume some of your time, but just think of the hours that will be freed up down the road for you to spend on your favorite pastimes. Cleaning off your desk can be the first step in the process of organizing your workspace, then your home, and eventually your entire life. Once you get used to living with one part of your life in a sane order where things can be located quickly, the ones that remain unorganized will seem woefully out of place, and the effort it takes to root around in their chaos will seem extremely time-consuming by comparison.

So even though it's like pulling teeth now, start cleaning off your desk and try to keep it clean because soon the rest of your unorganized life will follow suit. Here are a few ways to get started:

• Don't use your desk for storage purposes. That's what all those empty file cabinets are for. (You'll

F.Y.I.

One of the best ways to clean off your desk, or to rid yourself of excess horizontal surfaces, is to invest in a multifunction device that combines a printer, fax machine, copier, and even scanner in one compact machine. Not only will you free up space that you can use for more desktop filing systems, bins and baskets, but instead of having two or more pieces of high-tech equipment that each requires its own specific toner cartridge, when it comes time for maintenance, you'll only have to deal with one machine.

learn about filing systems in the next section.) If you have to put all of your computer equipment on your desk to prevent you from taking the easy way out by placing each new piece of paper on top of a growing stack instead of filing it, then do it. Commandeering the horizontal surface that is your desk with large bulky items is one way to remind yourself to get and then stay organized.

• Handle each piece of paper only once by assigning a priority to it and taking action the *first* time you pick it up. Take heart, though; you won't have to totally relinquish your piles. You'll simply replace them with baskets and desktop filing organizers, assigning a category to each one—things that need to be done today, letters that need to be written by the end of the week—as well as several out boxes, one to hold papers you want to keep in your own files and at least one to hold those you want to pass on to others. The secret to preventing these organizing bins from becoming substitutes for your "I'll Get to It Someday" piles is to set aside a time each day or each week to empty them by sending the papers and other documents on their way. Or, if you don't want to schedule a specific time, given your hectic and highly unpredictable schedule, you can sort them during those downtimes when you're waiting for a phone call or for a colleague to arrive for a meeting.

• Get in the habit of working with only one file or organizer at a time, and be sure to close it or set it aside before starting on another. Papers have a funny habit of jumping ship whenever our backs are turned. And they love to see what's happening with other pieces of paper to make sure they're not missing anything. To keep them where they belong, whenever you're sifting through a folder or sorting papers, make sure you keep them separated so that the papers in one file don't accidentally migrate to another.

Whenever you are holding a piece of paper in your hand, you have can react in one of three ways:

1. *Reply.* Perhaps a full-fledged letter is called for, or maybe you can get away with scrawling a handwritten note on a Post-it note or on a separate piece of notepaper.

2. *File.* If you need to hold on to the document for future reference, put it in its proper place immediately, whether it's a specific file folder or a basket designated to hold papers to be filed before the workweek is over.

3. *Throw it away.* This can be the toughest step to take. How could you possibly know now whether or not you'll need this information at some point in the future? Well, you can't, but the truth is that you probably won't need it. How often do you look for papers that you saved five or more years ago? If you're still nervous about tossing it, buy a scanner and put it on your desk. Scan anything you want to throw away, but *think* you may need. Then throw it away. It will take up a lot less room on a floppy disk or hard drive.

Filing Cabinets

If you don't have a lot of practice in organizing your life, but you *do* own a filing cabinet, no doubt

F.Y.I.

The average corporate executive receives 225 items of mail every month—and that's just the unsolicited mail. Each year, the average family receives about 200 catalogs that were not requested.

SMART SOURCES

Many stores that previously concentrated on selling housewares have found a lucrative niche in selling products that help organize the entire house.

Look for a local housewares store that has an extensive selection of organizational tools, or contact one of the following companies that do mail- and phone orders:

Space-Savers

This company has several stores in North Carolina, but it also accepts orders through its web site and ships anywhere.
336-722-8989
www.spacesavers.com

California Closets

California Closets is a franchised company with businesses located all over the United States and the world.
800-2SIMPLIFY
www.calclosets.com

purchased in one big whoosh of motivation one January 2, it probably serves the same purpose as the other horizontal surfaces in your office: it's a place for you to put towering stacks of paper until they fall over.

But now since you've started to read the *Smart Guide to Managing Your Time,* your thinking has changed. If you don't already have a filing cabinet, you'll need to go out and buy at least one to start with, or maybe several. If the subject is new to you—if you've never had to rely on a filing system that's well-organized and well-maintained—it may be difficult to decide what type and size to get. It's not necessary to run out and buy the biggest vertical file you can find. If, however, you think that the bottom drawer in your desk will be large enough to hold all of the papers and documents you've accumulated over the years, then it's a pretty good bet that you're underestimating the degree to which you've become seriously unorganized. So spring for at least a two-drawer freestanding model. And buy the sturdiest one you can find. It sounds silly, but some people who own one of the cheaper filing cabinets refuse to use it simply because they don't believe it will be able to stand up to their abuse.

It is also a good idea to go to the largest office-furniture store in your area for a complete selection. Filing cabinets come in all makes, models, and colors, and remember, it has to be something you want to use. So buy something you'll be happy with.

Next, you'll need to get the files that will store all your different types of papers and documents. Sounds simple, but there are a number of different components you'll need to pay attention to.

• *Hanging files.* These latch on to the steel bars that run the length of the file drawer. When it comes to how you'll use them to organize your papers, it may help to think of each hanging file as a book; for instance, for your tax records, one hanging file will contain all of your records for the tax year 1999.

• *File folders.* These are the manila or board folders that have tabs sticking out of the top. For filing purposes, file folders serve as the chapters in the book; these can be narrowed down by subject—like car expenses—or by month.

• *Plastic tabs with labels.* You'll use these to mark the hanging files. Using clear or colored tabs will help you to further categorize the contents of each file with an easy-to-reconize tab label.

• *Labels or markers in a variety of colors.* You can use these to stick or write on the tabs of the file folders to help you break things down further into categories, which will ultimately make it easier to find the papers you need.

When it comes to developing a system for filing, you know best about which names to give to your folders and files. Obviously, the clearer it is, the better, although you have to also make it easy to find. For instance, to organize papers from your college years, you may want to label the hanging file with the name of your college, although some people might instead categorize it by the years, by their major, or even by the type of degree they earned. Although you may occasionally ask another person—an assistant or coworker—to locate a document that you have filed and he may perhaps take a bit longer because he is looking for a file labeled

SMART DEFINITION

Vertical file cabinet

This is the most common type of file cabinet, and is widely available in two- or three-drawer models. Its drawers are deeper than they are wide. You can buy a vertical cabinet that holds the larger legal-size folders, where an 8-½ by 14 inch sheet of paper will fit easily, or the traditional kind, which is sized to fit a standard 8-½ by 11 inch piece of paper.

Lateral file cabinet

This type of file cabinet contains drawers that are wider than they are deep. Instead of storing your files face out, a lateral file cabinet stores them so they're arranged side by side. Like a vertical file cabinet, a lateral file cabinet comes in different sizes to store standard-size or legal-size files.

"Swarthmore College" while you may have labeled it "B.A./History," the important thing is to make it user-friendly for you, since you're the one who will be using it the most.

Shelving, Closets, and Long-Term Storage

For most people, even the biggest filing cabinet they can buy isn't big enough. Their space may be limited, or they have more things to store than they realized, or some of the items slated for storage are too large or too awkwardly shaped to fit into a file folder or on a desk. Or else, the item in question will fit nicely into the space you have, except that you need it so infrequently that having it within arm's length doesn't make much sense.

There is a wealth of choices available to organize the items that you want to have close at hand but still out of sight. Here are some of them:

• Stackable cardboard boxes will allow you to store unfiled papers and additional hanging file folders along with the awkwardly shaped items all in the same box—assuming you don't need to use it exclusively for your hanging files. You can squirrel these cartons away in a closet, under the bed, in a hallway, or even behind a piece of furniture.

• Contrary to popular belief, a closet is not a black hole in which to toss everything you don't think you'll need in the next week. You'll be able to fit at least twice as much of your stuff in a spare closet if you take the time to organize it first. Go to a home-design store to see the selection of hanging organizers, lazy susan devices for clothes, shoes, or even papers and files, and panels that divide a closet into separate areas.

• Adding just a couple of bookshelves on the wall where their contents can be seen is a great way to organize your books and other bulky items while making use of wall space that would otherwise be wasted. Arrange the shelves the same way you would label hanging files and folders; for example, you might devote each shelf to a particular subject or category—of book, paper, or other item— to make it easy for you to find items later on.

There are two reasons why the number of self-storage businesses in this country has skyrocketed since 1990: people don't have enough room in their homes and apartments for their seldom-used items, plus they just keep accumulating more stuff despite having no place to store it. Renting a self-storage unit can be cheaper than building an addition onto your house or moving into a bigger house, especially if you're not sure if you're going to stay in your present house for more than a couple of years.

If you're trying to decide whether to rent a self-storage unit, make sure the facility you're considering is secure and well lit, and provides access during the times you think you'll need to get to it. You should plan to store only those items you won't be needing more often than once a month, especially if the facility is more than a short drive from your house. You usually have your choice of various storage unit sizes. Because the larger sizes are more expensive, you will probably want to start out with the smallest size you estimate will be able

F.Y.I.

It probably won't surprise you to find out that the number of self-storage businesses has grown rapidly in the last thirty years. In fact, self-storage is now a $5 billion industry with a trade organization, the Self Storage Association, a publication called the *Self Storage Legal Review,* and even an annual convention and trade show. Although the vast majority of self-storage businesses are scrupulous, be sure to do your homework before entrusting your valuables to a self-storage business.

Of course, as you go through the process of throwing out as much as you can to clear some space in your home or office, there are some things you need to save, like financial and tax records, for instance. It's a common fact that the Internal Revenue Service reserves the right to conduct an audit of any tax return you've filed up to seven years ago. As a result, accountants and auditors alike suggest that you hold on to canceled checks, pay stubs, receipts, and bank account statements for at least three years before tossing them. Some even recommend you save them for up to seven years, which proves that you can never be too cautious when it comes to the IRS.

to hold all the items that you plan to store—but be sure to arrange for a move-up clause that will allow you to graduate to the next size without penalty, in case you uncover more stuff back home that you'd like to get out from underfoot.

Another Option: Throw It Out!

Remember the days when your most prized possessions consisted of a dog-eared copy of *The Catcher in the Rye* and a candle stub saved from the Chianti bottle from your first dinner with a now long-forgotten date? Now look around at your surroundings: how on earth did you go from having just a few worldly possessions to owning so much stuff?

It's not too difficult: after all, ours is a society that strives to cherish and collect material things. And the more, the better, in most instances. You've seen how you can run into trouble when you start to sort papers that you've held onto for decades, so how do you decide which possessions you can part with and which you can keep? And how do you convince your spouse or partner that you'll never throw out your 1967 Superman comic book?

Even a traditional and thorough spring cleaning binge leaves a lot of stuff behind in attics, garages, and hall closets that you don't really need. It's the brave ones who are able to have a huge garage or apartment sale, or else swallow hard and donate the whole pile to the Salvation Army or Goodwill and not look back. Of course, there will always be a few things you'll want to keep for sentimental reasons. And you should be prepared to do a bit of bargaining so that you can hold on to an object of yours that your spouse considers to be worthless, and vice versa. But be prepared to get ruthless: after all, why do you need to hang on to a ten-year-old word-processing manual for a program you stopped using five years ago? Whatever you hang on to, just make sure it makes sense. Imagine that it has to justify the space it's taking up by paying rent and ask yourself, would it still be worth it?

Your Work Area: The Big Picture

It's a generally accepted dictum of professional chefs that when they're working in their kitchens, every item that they will need should be within arm's reach of one central point, which is usually directly in front of the stove. This allows a chef to turn ninety degrees to the right and left, but with a minimum of movement, since space in most professional kitchens is at a premium, and there is nearly always another staff member nearby to get in the way.

When planning the space that you work in, you'll need to plot out the same measure of efficiency and quality. Whether you're rethinking your workspace in your office or want to furnish a spare room in your house so you can do your drawing and painting, the most important—and often overlooked—aspect is adequate light. Even before you consider the ergonomics of your work

SMART SOURCES

For more information about how to properly position your office equipment as well as your body, check out the following book and mail-order resources:

Repetitive Strain Injury: A Computer User's Guide by Emil Pascarelli and Deborah Quilter
Ergonomics, Inc.
www.ergonomicsinc.com

area, you'll need to analyze the lighting. The lighting in your workspace should be bright enough so that you don't have to strain your eyes or your body in order to see what you're working on, but not so bright that the glare is hurtful or tiring to your eyes. Ideally you should have at least two sources of light, one illuminating your immediate work area and one providing general illumination to prevent shadows on the documents you're viewing. If you're working at a computer, any light that comes through a window should be at your back, and not shining in your eyes. If you plan to work at night, a desk lamp will help illuminate documents on your desk that may be difficult to see under an overhead light.

The air that surrounds you is also an important part of workspace planning that frequently gets overlooked. Though comfort temperature is a personal matter—some like it hot, others like it cold—most people prefer a room filled with fresh air that is constantly circulating to a stuffy, closed-in room where a lack of fresh air makes it difficult to concentrate for long periods of time.

Sometimes a stuffy room can be aired out by simply opening a window. However, as many high-rise office buildings and apartment complexes have windows that can't be opened, this is impossible for a large number of workers. If the stale air in your workplace prevents you from working at your peak, sometimes a simple desk fan is enough to circulate the air and bring some relief. Some people find that electronic air ionizers and refreshers do the trick. In any case, taking a brisk walk outdoors during your lunch hour or break will help clear the cobwebs from your brain and make it easier for you to concentrate on your work back at the office.

The desk where you work should be situated so that it is easy to reach all parts of the top surface by just swiveling your chair, and not by having to crane your neck or stretch at an uncomfortable angle. Some people prefer to have a simple desk, while others prefer an angled work surface in the shape of an "L" or a "U" in order to spread out their projects and papers.

You'll need to make sure that your chair, desk, and computer equipment are positioned at a comfortable angle to minimize strain on your joints and tendons. The incidence of carpal tunnel syndrome and other repetitive stress injuries has reached epidemic proportions in some industries, especially in jobs where employees are required to use a computer for long periods of time. If your work subjects you to this kind of stress, there are a number of things that you can do to protect your hands:

• Take frequent breaks. Type or work for five to ten minutes at a time, and then rest and stop using your hands. Read, pet a nearby cat, or get up and walk around.

• Make sure that your chair is positioned properly as well as your hands and monitor.

• If your hands or forearms start to get sore or numb or they begin to tingle, stop working. Stretch your fingers back, massage the sore spots, or apply an ice pack.

• Try wearing wrist splints to help remind you to keep your hands in the correct position. Be aware, however, that they don't work for everyone.

WHAT MATTERS, WHAT DOESN'T

What Matters

• Having papers, books, and equipment organized and within reach so you can find them quickly.

• Taking pride that you can be creative and well-organized.

• Realizing that if you experience a temporary lapse in judgment and stop filing your papers, you'll get back on track.

What Doesn't

• Being overly obsessive about being able to locate any document in five seconds or less.

• Thinking that organizing and cleaning up your home and workspace will ruin your reputation.

• Figuring that if you temporarily get buried by paper, you might as well throw in the towel and revert to your formerly messy state.

Keep in mind that when it comes to setting up the area where you'll be working, it's the combination of the tools, the furniture, and the environment around you that will help keep you healthy and your mind clear. You may have to tinker with each aspect for awhile before you stumble onto the perfect combination that works best for you.

Making sure that the spaces you work and play in suit your temperament, your projects, and your own personal work style can take a lot of planning and time, and when it comes to your budget, truly the sky can be the limit. Because of this, the act of planning and organizing your space can easily consume the largest amount of time of any of the strategies you'll put into play as a result of reading the *Smart Guide to Managing Your Time*. But once you have your physical space in order, you'll feel empowered to tackle the rest of the factors that are preventing you from managing your time properly.

In the following chapter, you'll add a few more arrows to your quiver of time-management tools—tools that not only can streamline your life but are also fun to work with.

....

Time-Management Tools

Okay, you have reached the halfway point of the book, and by now you have learned a little about how to manage your time and organize your space more efficiently. And you've resolved to do even more to make your life run even more smoothly. Congratulations!

As you'll discover in this chapter, there are a bevy of tools designed to help you to do just this. You can try them out one at a time, and either combine them all to turn yourself into a streamlined smoothly running machine, or favor just one or two, turning to the others on special occasions.

To-Do Lists

Even if you've always considered yourself to be totally unorganized, chances are that you've used at least some form of to-do list in the past, whether scribbled in haste on a napkin in a diner when you remembered the errands you needed to run before heading back to the office, or meticulously outlined and numbered, with the tasks rated in order of their importance.

If you've previously scrawled down the tasks on whatever was handy as they popped into your mind, then it's no wonder why later you couldn't find the napkin, back of an envelope, or subscription blow-out card that you wrote them on.

Now is the time for you to get serious and make the most of your to-do list. First, if you're currently using some kind of to-do list, what do you primarily use it for: work tasks, home-related tasks, or both? And if you do combine them on one list, do you write them down in the order they come to mind, or the order in which you'll perform them as you head around town?

When you create your to-do list, think about the kind of life you lead, the route you take back and forth to work, as well as the kinds of projects that are currently on your agenda, both at home and at the office. Would it make sense to draw up one list that incorporates all the things that you need to do that day, or would it be better for you to make two separate lists, one devoted solely to work-related tasks and the other to home-oriented responsibilities, or perhaps one for the morning and another for the afternoon and evening? You may want to keep one pad or notebook and split it down the middle or buy two and delegate specific kinds of tasks to each. Of course, appointments and meetings will go into your datebook or personal digital assistant—the types and variations of these tools will be explored next—so that your to-do list is freed up for the actual tasks you need to accomplish.

Another way to plan your to-do list is to separate the items into categories of tasks you normally do. For instance, you may want to divide the list into columns: one for phone calls you have to make, another for letters and notes you need to send, and a third for actions you need to take on certain projects, from scheduling a meeting to returning a library book.

Once you decide which format would work best for you, then head for the stationery store. Perhaps one reason why you haven't kept your to-do list up to date in the past is because it's been boring, or resembled your other notebooks, pads and ledgers, and got buried as a result. Here is your excuse to be outrageous, to have fun and choose a format that you'll want to use. Whether that means buying

STREET SMARTS

If you feel constricted by keeping your to-do list down to a page or two, or limiting it to one week's projects, do what one woman does: make a longer to-do list!

The difference between hers and the one-page variety is that hers contains every single thing she wants to do in her life. She prioritizes every activity, however, and moves items around as she crosses off completed tasks. If you use a long list, keep it in a word-processing file, with each page headlined as to time frame—"Today," "This Week," "This Year," and so on. This may just be the best solution for people who are always thinking about the next project on their list.

SMART SOURCES

If you like to hold onto mementos and assorted papers of sentimental value, why not start a scrapbook, or a memory book, where you can keep cards, notes, match-books, and other keepsakes. Here are some good sources:

Scrapbooking Idea Network

An Internet resource center. www.scrapbooking.com

Keeping Memories Alive

Everything for the scrapbook maker. 800-419-4949 www.scrapbooks.com

Creative Memories

Independent consul-tants who hold home scrapbook parties. 800-468-9335 www.creative-memories.com

a special pad with hot-pink paper or a notebook with a Mickey Mouse cover, go for it. While you're at it, spring for a box of magic markers or crayons so that you can even color-code your to-do list. Also pick up a couple pads of Post-it notes in wild colors so you can add items to your list as your day proceeds. To help you prioritize the tasks you write down, buy a few sheets of stickers, whether gold stars, animals, or cartoon characters.

One thing to watch when your agenda involves long projects is that the items you write down on your to-do list are manageable chunks of the overall project. Make them as specific as possible. "Finish Smith project" is too broad. "Write Jones summary in Smith project" is better. When task items are not specific enough, they can often seem so overwhelming that the list becomes self-defeating from the start.

The point is to make creating and maintaining a to-do list so much fun that you can't help but want to work on it. After all, with a to-do list, as with the other time management tools described in this chapter, if you don't pick the tool up and actually use it, you're just wasting your money and, more importantly, your time.

Datebooks

The widespread use of such ubiquitous datebooks and personal agendas as Day-Timers and Day Runners has made so many people so dependent on their daily planners that some feel lost if their planner is not by their side where they can see it at all times.

As is the case with the other time-management

tools described in this chapter, the specific style of datebook you select will be largely a personal decision. Your preferences for color, feel, cover, and layout of the pages will all play a part in your decision.

Datebooks come in a variety of formats and sizes. Some spread one week across two pages, while others have a separate page for each day, or even two pages to one day. Most busy people feel that trying to squeeze a full week of activities—for yourself and for your family—into two relatively small pages would be an exercise in futility. What is perhaps better is to have at least one page allotted for each day, though if you tend to scribble notes to yourself and not leave enough room to fit in appointments, the two-pages-a-day format would probably work better for you.

In addition to general-purpose datebooks, some are specially designed and marketed to executives, both male and female, while others are aimed at artists, mothers, teachers, doctors, and so on. And some datebooks even contain a page for each day where you can jot down your to-do list, which eliminates yet another pad or journal for you to carry around and keep track of.

Many of the day-to-day datebooks also contain a month-at-a-glance page that is placed at the beginning of each new month. Here, you may want to transfer the schedule from your large wall calendar described in the following section, or just clip a copy directly into the book.

Here are some tips that will help you manage your datebook as efficiently as possible:

• No matter how many things you need to accomplish in the course of a single day, remember to leave yourself some breathing room. Many people think that in order to get the most out of each day,

SMART SOURCES

If you're looking for software that will help you draw up your to-do list, check out the products from the following companies. You can download a demo version of their software from their web pages and try before you buy:

Day Runner

Day Runner produces the Day Runner Planner for Windows that allows you to create a to-do list, and then print it out so you can place it in your Day Runner organizer. 800-643-9923 www.dayrunner.com

Day-Timer

Day-Timer Organizer Version 2.1 is the most popular brand—based on the number of units sold—and allows you to place all of your tasks into the program and then categorize them by priority. 800-225-5005 www.daytimer.com

they need to schedule back-to-back appointments and meetings, with no room to spare. As you have already learned, everyone needs some downtime built into his or her day, whether it is intentional or accidental. Besides, you can't plan for traffic jams and other events that will derail your schedule, so try to leave at least twenty minutes between appointments.

• A few months into using your datebook, it may be crammed with papers, notes, tickets, and other items you need to get to in a hurry. For this reason, you may want to choose a datebook that contains plastic zippered envelopes, pockets, or built-in file folders so that you don't lose any stray papers. A datebook designed with a binder system makes it easy to move pages around. For instance, if your datebook has an address book in the back, but you use it so much that you'd prefer it in the front, a loose-leaf binder makes it easy to switch the position.

• Make sure your datebook is always nearby, and that it is open to the current day. After all, it can't help you remember the meetings and appointments you schedule if you can't see them written down.

• Whenever you schedule an appointment, make sure that you write down all the pertinent information that you'll need next to the appointment time. Log the contact's name, address, and phone number, along with clear directions to the location if you haven't been there before; directions written on a separate sheet of paper are too easily lost or otherwise separated from your datebook. Any specific meeting agenda is also helpful.

Calendars

If your datebook is the "trees," helping you keep on top of the myriad details that fill your life, then your monthly calendar is the "forest," the big picture. Because it is so easy to get distracted and bogged down by the details, it's a good idea to make your calendar as big as possible. A pocket-sized calendar with one month to a page won't be of much help because it's easy to misplace, and important dates will have the tendency to slide by.

Instead, get a large wall calendar, or at least a desk blotter that's big enough so you'll be able to write things like QUARTERLY REPORT DUE on a particular date and still be able to see it across the room without squinting. You can get a traditional paper model, or a vinyl wall calendar that allows you to fill in the blanks with the months and days with a quick-erase pen. You can even purchase a quick-erase model that covers three months, which will help you keep long-range plans in mind. If you have the wall space available, getting both a three-month and a month-by-month calendar will give you no excuse to forget about projects that are due a couple of months down the road.

As with your to-do list, be creative and have fun with your calendar by using colored markers, stickers, Post-it notes, and other visual items to help you keep to your current schedule and stay aware of all your upcoming deadlines. If you have a number of different projects, or if other people are using the same calendar, assign each project or person a different colored marker. This way, it's easy to keep track of your own projects as well as know if a colleague will be available to help you out in a pinch.

Here are some tips to help you make your calendar into as useful a time-management tool as possible:

• When you write down an appointment in your datebook, be sure to write it down on your calendar as well. This will help remind you of the meeting while you let others know about your previous commitments.

• Make copies of your calendar to keep in other locations where you may need to refer to it. These may include your home, your partner or spouse's office, even your car. With a copy machine you can shrink it down so that it's no larger than a page, but you can still read the entries clearly.

• People change; so do their calendars. If you suddenly find yourself bored by your calendar, don't hesitate to switch to another style or format in the middle of the year. Remember, you want to do whatever it takes so that your calendar and other time-management tools remain useful in helping you keep your life on track. If something no longer works for whatever reason, feel free to find something that does.

• Don't feel compelled to fill every block in your calendar when you first put it up. Even though you may be managing your time more efficiently, you may still view long blocks of empty space on your calendar as a threat. Before you start filling in those days, however, think about your own schedule and how you rarely seem to have trouble filling it up with just the day-to-day tasks. If you schedule events just to fill up the days three months hence, you'll likely be overbooked when that day finally arrives.

Besides using the standard time-management tools already described in this chapter, consider using other things to help you manage your time and get your work done. Here are some ideas:

• Keep a chalkboard next to your wall calendar so you can use it to "think out loud" and consider several different scenarios before committing one of them to the calendar.

• Turn one entire wall in a hallway into a bulletin board or idea center. Get a roll of butcher paper and line a wall, or mount a large erasable board and encourage people to express their opinions, provide constructive criticism about work, or voice their thoughts on the world, current events, or work. Consider it to be a place to blow off steam.

High-Tech Time-Management Tricks

You can buy a wide variety of software programs that accomplish the same things as traditional paper planners, calendars, and to-do lists. While some people are technophobes who would never dream of trading in their old-fashioned way of keeping track of their schedule, others, who have to have the newest version of any kind of software they use, snap up the latest and greatest in time-management and day-planning software the minute it hits the stores or becomes available for download from the manufacturer's Web site.

Of course, any kind of technology can thwart even your most sincere efforts at efficiently man-

F.Y.I.

Sometimes it's the simple things that work best. Because you may not always have access to a pad and paper, or don't feel comfortable jotting on a pad when you're driving on the freeway, get in the habit of dictating thoughts and ideas into a tape recorder. You can include items for your to-do list, compose letters or e-mail to friends you haven't heard from in a while, or even make out your shopping list.

aging your time—how many times have you
responded to a fax or e-mail just minutes after you
received it, because of the urgency that faxes and
e-mail convey? After all, it is possible to spend
more time tinkering with your schedule in an
electronic format than the amount of time you
would save by using it in the first place and then
leaving it alone. However, time-management software can help you to accomplish everything that
other organizational tools can, once you learn
how to use them. And remember that you may
still have to print out a hard copy.

The advantage of learning to use any kind of
computer is the amount of time you'll save on performing rudimentary grunt work, like printing out
endless personalized letters. The downside is that
the vast majority of people never learn everything
that a particular program can do for them. To get
the most out of your software, you may want to
locate the manufacturer's Web site, go to technical
support, and as a registered user of the program
(you do register all new software you purchase,
right?), ask how their software can help you to
accomplish a certain task. You may want to look at
the company's standard files and FAQs before you
send off an e-mail to tech support. That way, you
can get your information without having to wait
for a tech advisor to get back to you.

If you find that you're jotting down lots of
notes when you're on the road, only to have to
enter them into your computer when you get
back to the office or home, you may want to invest
in a laptop to save you from having to record
information twice. If you use a laptop to write
down notes, you can easily transfer the file to your
desktop system. A laptop will also allow you to go
online when you're away from the office to check

your e-mail or locate a fact or other information on a Web site you've visited in the past.

Some of the best ways to use your computer to help you manage your time better are also the easiest: they involve common sense and regular maintenance of your computer system. Here are some smart tips that you should follow, no matter how you use your hardware and software:

• Back up your software and hard drive on a regular basis, and be sure to write down the date of the backup in your datebook. Some experts recommend that you perform a backup of new files and programs every week, and of your entire hard drive at least once a month. Investigate some of the tape backup systems available as well as off-site storage possibilities.

• If your hard drive is taking longer to locate and load programs and files, you may need to run a defragmentation program on your drive. Fragmentation occurs because your hard drive often has to break larger files into smaller fragments, storing each piece where it will fit. As a result, the data in one file may be scattered all across your hard drive. Some defragging programs to try include Norton Utilities, DiskExpress, or the one tucked inside the Windows system folder.

• Due to the increased use of e-mail, shared files, and downloaded attachments, more viruses are being spread to more computer systems. Every computer you use should contain an antivirus program, which will alert if a virus is present on any file, program, or e-mail that enters your system. Some good antivirus programs include VirusScan and Norton Anti-Virus.

F.Y.I.

The first software program designed to help people organize their time better was called Agenda, manufactured by the Lotus Development Corporation in the early 1980s. The founder of Lotus, Mitch Kapor, developed Agenda because he was searching for a high-tech way to organize himself. Kapor also referred to Agenda as a personal information manager, or PIM.

SMART SOURCES

Compare products and prices of high-tech tools online, through an 800 number, and office supply stores. A few for you to explore:

Applied Computer Online Services

Carries more than 300,000 products and more than 110,000 software programs that can be downloaded from their web site. 888-927-7543 www.applied-computer.com

Computer Discount Warehouse

A Fortune 1000 company named as one of the world's top ten catalog companies. 800-848-4239 www.cdw.com

PC Connection

Offers 24-hour ordering and overnight shipping. Its sister company, Mac Connection, sells everything for the Mac. 800-800-0009 www.pcconnection.com

Electronic Organizers

Whether they're referred to as personal information managers or PDAs (personal digital assistants), electronic organizers can provide an all-in-one computerized solution to just about all of your time-management problems. Because of their size (they are smaller than a laptop), they don't allow you to store as much information. However, they can still take care of the bulk of the things that you'll need when you're away from your primary desktop system, and when you see what they can do, you'll know why they have caught on so quickly.

Electronic organizers, also known as palmtops, boast a variety of time-management skills. They will allow you to store your Rolodex and phone and address books, your appointment calendar, your to-do list, and various files for keeping notes. But they don't stop there. You can also send e-mail and faxes through wireless modes—that is, you don't have to be connected to a telephone to connect to your Internet service provider. You can drag and drop information—from your address book, for instance, to your appointment calendar. Many models offer you the ability to jot down a few notes or even to create a rough sketch on what resembles a touch pad, which it will then translate to a word-processing or graphics file.

With an electronic organizer, you can also create tickler files to set off an alarm to remind you of an upcoming appointment; install additional programs, like a map for a city you're planning to visit; and effortlessly transfer any file to your desktop computer. Most electronic organizers also contain a calculator, a dictionary, a thesaurus, and conversion charts, among other useful directories.

The downside is that you can become overly reliant on a PDA. Of course, this isn't necessarily bad, but it could prove disastrous if your electronic organizer is the only place where you store important information and you haven't backed up the data by transferring it to a laptop or desktop computer. Also, the keypads provided with palmtops are, well, palm-sized. You won't be able to input information at your regular fast clip. Early models tended to crash easily and regularly, and the screens on some models frequently leave users with a nasty case of eyestrain. Plus, as with any popular piece of portable electronic equipment, your PDA can become a target for thieves; if it's lost or stolen and you haven't transferred your data to another computer system, you'll have to recreate all of your information and files from scratch.

With that said, you should still take some time to decide whether a palmtop would work for you. While they haven't created the same kind of revolution in our lives that the PC has, electronic organizers have pushed the envelope when it comes to mobility and portability issues. As is always the case with new developments in technology, there's lots of excitement when a new piece of equipment is introduced that can do something that its predecessors couldn't. But there will always be a sleek new computerized *something* just around the bend that will radically improve your life. What you should decide is, will this new item make managing your life even a little bit easier? If you answer yes, then consider the cost and whether you can afford it, as well as the learning curve that is involved. Then, if all's well, you should spring for it.

SMART MONEY

As is the case with computers and peripherals, the prices of most high-tech equipment have dropped precipitously in just a brief period of time. For example, a top-of-the-line Hewlett-Packard flatbed scanner that sold for $1300 in 1996 cost a mere $75 in late 1998.

Most computer retailers, of course, want you to purchase a piece of high-tech equipment the first time you walk in the store, but secretly they'll advise that if you don't need it immediately, then waiting even a few months will enable you to take advantage of a significant price drop.

Voice Recognition, Scanners, and Other Fun Stuff

This is the kind of stuff that causes some people to shake their heads and say, "It's magic, right out of the Jetsons."

Voice-recognition software, scanners, and other high-tech tools that let you get your work done faster and easier have caught the attention of the American public like wildfire, in part because they seem to be straight out of a science fiction novel of the 1950s or even the 1970s. Voice-recognition software—Via Voice and Naturally Speaking are two popular examples—works like this: You speak as if you are giving dictation into a tiny but powerful microphone that's attached to a headset. As you speak, your words pass through the special voice-recognition programming, and then your words are transferred to a word-processing file. While you talk, each word appears on the computer screen before your eyes.

Of course, you first have to train the software to respond to the sound of your voice, your volume, your accent, and your pronunciation of certain words. However, once you have gone through the initial training session, the accuracy rate is about 95 percent; meaning that for every twenty words you speak, one will come up on the word-processing screen as something that's slightly different from what you said. And as you continue to use the software to dictate letters, write books, and create other documents, the voice-recognition program fine-tunes itself even more, pushing the accuracy rate closer to 100 percent.

Much like voice-recognition software, scanners eliminate the process of typing or of painstakingly recreating a photo or illustration by hand or by screening an image with photographic equipment and then cutting and pasting it into a document. You place a document—either a piece of writing or a photo or illustration—on the scanner, which then takes a picture of it in the same way a copy machine duplicates a document. Text data is then processed by character-recognition software and transfered into a word-processing document. With art and illustrations, the scanning software sends the scanned image into a photo illustration or graphics software program, which which allows you to alter the image in many different ways.

Scanners come in two forms: one looks like a flatbed copier, and the other is a device that feeds the paper you want scanned through its rollers. There are also handheld portable devices that you run over the surface of a page or sheet of paper, but the accuracy rate depends on the stillness of your hand and your ability to hold the scanner perfectly straight so that it doesn't scan the words at an angle.

The great benefit of both voice-recognition software and scanners is that they drastically cut down on the amount of time you would otherwise spend typing the data into your computer. If you tend to strain your hands and wrists from too much typing and are at risk for developing carpal tunnel syndrome or another repetitive strain injury, these items almost make it unnecessary to type. But they're not for everybody, or for every use.

For one, since speech tends to be looser and to ramble more than writing, chances are that a letter or document that you "write" by dictating it into voice-recognition software will turn out differently

WHAT MATTERS, WHAT DOESN'T

What Matters
• Investigating new technology to see if it would reduce your workload or increase the quality or quantity of your work.

• Spending time with a new PDA or other piece of high-tech equipment to learn about the scope of what it can accomplish for you.

• Shopping around not only to get the best price but to get good service when your equipment needs maintenance or repair.

What Doesn't
• Rushing to buy new equipment as soon as it arrives in stores.

• Slavishly tinkering with high-tech equipment to shave a few seconds off your work.

• Buying at the lowest prices you can find, regardless of the warranties, store, or manufacturer.

than if you typed that same document into the word-processing program yourself. However, the photo illustration programs—like PhotoShop and PaintShop Pro—actually allow a lot more leeway and creativity in altering an image to the way you really want it to appear.

As you're discovering, though voice-recognition software and scanners can save you a lot of work and time, they still won't do everything for you. But they will free you up enough so that you'll have more time to spend on the things that really matter: creating and thinking.

Undoubtedly, there will be new technological devices, software, and other developments that will come down the pike, all purporting to be the latest and greatest and claiming to save you buckets of time, enough so that you'll be able to earn a Ph.D. in just one year. Evaluate each new offering that appeals to you to see if it will save you valuable time, and give it a try if it seems promising. If, however, after a trial period, it appears to consume more time than it's worth, then give it up.

You've learned about a wide variety of the tools that are available to help you to efficiently manage your time and schedule. You've also discovered that the tools you choose should be easy to learn, powerful, and fun so that you want to use them.

Now it's time to get down to serious business and find out about even more tools you can use and behavior you can employ in many specific but common situations at work and at home.

THE BOTTOM LINE

Any tool you can find to help you to organize your life and manage your time better—whether high-tech or low-tech—will do wonders to streamline your life and even improve your outlook.

But don't buy something just because a magazine, an expert or a friend tells you it's the greatest thing since sliced bread. Take the time to research and experiment with it to make sure that it fits your specific lifestyle and needs. If it's a poor match, you'll end up wasting time instead of saving it.

Time Management at Work

How many times has the following happened to you: You wake up in the morning raring to go and actually eager to get to work so you can dig in on a new project. Once you arrive, you start to lose yourself in the work only to get interrupted by an "urgent" phone call, an unexpected meeting, or a coworker who stops in uninvited, just wanting to chat. You'd like to get back to work, but you don't want to seem rude. As a result, all of your desire and good intentions fly out the window.

Learning how to effectively manage your time at work is like walking a tightrope: although you have to get your work done, you also have to give your attention to urgent matters that sometimes seem as if they are trying to derail your day and workload on purpose.

Here's how to deal with them while remaining cordial and diplomatic.

Dealing with the Phone

A constantly ringing telephone can be one of the biggest time wasters when you're in an office environment. And if you decide to let voicemail pick up so you can get in a few uninterrupted hours of work, then later deal with returning all of your phone messages, possibly only to leave messages on other people's voicemail and then waiting for them to return your call, you can start to feel as if you've entered into some kind of voicemail funhouse, especially when it seems there's only voice messages and not a "person" to speak with.

The problem arises because many people perceive a ringing phone as an urgent signal that has to be answered immediately. They believe that if they're sitting there, they should interrupt whatever they're working on and pick up the receiver instead of letting the answering machine or voicemail handle it. This is one of the most common ways that people allow their workdays to run away from them, so that at the end of the day they're left wondering how the day flew by without much work getting accomplished.

Here are a few tips to help you make the most of your phone time while making more time for the important things you need to get done:

• Whenever you leave a voicemail message, let the person know when you'll be answering the phone. It's also a good idea on your outgoing voicemail message to let people know the specific times that you do pick up the phone. If you can switch your voicemail between two different messages—one for when you're working, and the other for your open phone time, to let people know you're there but that you're on the other line—this may prove to be a satisfactory solution.

• Set aside a particular time of your day to make outgoing phone calls. Some people batch their phone calls in mid- to late afternoon when other people are probably reaching the end of their attention span, while others make them first thing in the morning when their thinking is clearest and they know they'll be able to accomplish their business in less time. No matter what time you choose, make sure you stick to it, and don't make calls at other times of the day unless it's urgent or you know you can keep the call short.

STREET SMARTS

Lely Barea runs Ibiley Uniforms, a school-uniform wholesale and retail operation in Miami, and relies on cell phones to keep in touch with her managers at six stores and at the manufacturing plant in Santo Domingo. She uses the phones to delegate and a personal digital assistant to keep detailed notes on each manager as well as most employees.

She believes that personal communication is crucial to growing the business. Although she has an office at corporate headquarters, she spends most of her time on the road meeting with managers and dealing with problems that crop up unexpectedly by communicating via cell phone. Each of her four children is also equipped with a cell phone so that each can contact her at anytime.

• Arrange to use some of your lengthier phone calls as actual phone "meetings": schedule a specific time for them, plan a particular agenda for discussion, and try to keep the conversation from getting sidetracked.

• When you reach the person you're calling, the first thing you should say is that your time is limited: "I just have a few minutes, but I wanted to check this out with you . . ."

• Equally important is to ask if it's convenient for your caller to talk with you when you phone. This will show consideration and acknowledge the other person's busy schedule.

• Get rid of call waiting. It has to be one of the rudest inventions ever created: in essence, it allows you to tell the person you're talking with that the incoming call may be more important than your current conversation. Instead, get voicemail that will be activated by an incoming call if you're already on the phone.

• Another way to show your consideration for others is to make the voicemail messages you leave as brief as possible. Think of the times someone left a long, rambling message on your voicemail, and how you rolled your eyes in response. Don't give someone else the excuse to do the same when you call. Announce your name, say your piece, leave information on how and when to contact you, and then hang up.

• Here's an easy, but frequently overlooked aspect of voicemail messages: smile when you're talking. People will notice the difference.

Cell Phone Etiquette

Because cell phones have erupted upon the American scene in such a big way in such a short time, people haven't learned what constitutes proper cell phone etiquette. Here's what the sixteenth edition of *Emily Post's Etiquette* has to say on the subject:

• Answer your phone or pager promptly so it doesn't annoy those around you. If you are going to a performance or a public event, deactivate it or put it on vibrate mode.

• If you're going to a public event, and you really don't need to be instantly accessible, leave that phone or pager at home.

• If you must take or make a call in public, remove yourself to a quiet corner where you won't bother others. If this isn't possible, speak quietly. It isn't proper to ask others to hush so you can hear.

• If you are paged and must respond immediately, excuse yourself (if necessary). Those with you shouldn't try to impede or criticize your need to find a phone.

Knock, Knock! Can I Come In?

Uh-oh, it is yet another of your coworkers knocking on your door—whether it's open or shut—asking for a few minutes of your time. Of course you know what happens: a few minutes turns into a half hour, then more people poke their heads in as they're walking by, and before you know it, instead of having the morning to work under deadline on an important project, your office has turned into one big kaffeeklatsch with you as host,

STREET MONEY

One of the reasons you may allow an interruption to command your attention is because the project you are working on isn't that intriguing to begin with.

As the novelist Robert Benchley said, "Anyone can do any amount of work, provided it isn't the work he is supposed to be doing at that moment."

Prove Benchley wrong by taking many of the suggestions in this book to heart: learn to delegate certain tasks so you can work on those that really interest you. And when you have to work on projects that can get pretty tedious, try our suggestions for overcoming procrastination—among them, "Just one-two-three, bungee!"

a forced smile on your face and your blood pressure rapidly rising because you don't want to be rude by asking everyone to leave.

In today's workplace, it's virtually impossible to prevent or foresee every interruption that is comes down the pike and straight for your office. And of course, you want to be available to help out in urgent situations, like those times when you suddenly realize the deadline for a new or prospective client became garbled somewhere along the line, and the report is due tomorrow, not next week as you had originally planned.

But you need at least one block of uninterrupted time each day, when you know you are free to give your undivided attention to a person or project. Here are some ways to cope:

• If at all possible, close your door and let everyone know that is a sign not to disturb you for any reason, unless the building is on fire. If you don't have a door, hang a sign on your cubicle with the same conditions.

• As is the case with your phone calls, arrange to have prescheduled times of the day when people can contact you with questions or for help.

• If someone barges into your office, stays longer than you want, and ignores all of your pointed glances at your watch, stand up and start moving towards the door to escort them out.

• If you can't prevent coworkers from interrupting you, then try to come in early or stay late in order to get some of your work done. Or else you can bring it home or arrange to telecommute for at least one day a week.

• Train yourself to say, "I'm busy," while offering an alternative time to meet and talk.

• If there is another employee who can help a chronic interrupter with a problem, then personally escort her to the other person's office, saying, "I'd love to help, but I'm just too busy."

Keeping a written log of the interruptions that arise throughout the course of a day can help you take control of your time. Write down the person's name, the purpose of the interruption, the time when it occurred and the amount of time it took, and whether the problem was solved or just postponed. If you begin to see a pattern—that is, the same people tend to interrupt you at the same time every day—you can train yourself to expect them and head them off at the pass. You can either be away from your desk on another errand or get up from your desk a minute or two before they are scheduled to make their appearance, and make sure they aren't able to get into your office.

Of course, if a chronic interrupter persists in distracting you from your work, remember the old adage, if you can't beat 'em, join 'em. Hand a pile of envelopes that need stuffing or reports that need collating to the perpetrator and say, "As long as you're here, you might as well help me." One of two things will happen: you'll be able to get twice the work done in the same amount of time, or else the interrupter will think long and hard before he interrupts you again, and your problem is solved . . . until the next interruption-prone coworker crosses your threshold.

F.Y.I.

The worst time to catch someone on the phone tends to be Monday mornings from 9 A.M. to 11 A.M., which is when many people are rested up from the weekend and eager to dive right into their work. Of course, what frequently happens is that you end up playing telephone tag for the remainder of the week if you're unable to reach a person on the first try.

High-Tech Interruptions

With the advent and omnipresence of pagers, cell phones, portable fax machines, and e-mail, many people are secure in the knowledge that they are inseparably connected to the outside world via their assortment of high-tech umbilical cords. In some cases, the endless rings and beeps help to boost the person's ego, making her feel important and indispensable; otherwise, she asks, why would all these people want to get in touch with me?

However, for people who are trying to make a concentrated effort to manage their time better, these disruptions can be an unwelcome and annoying distraction. The sheer urgency with which these devices announce themselves to the world is akin to an alarm clock's shrill demand!

E-mail can be a particular problem, especially if you subscribe to mailing lists and receive incoming mail one letter at a time instead of in a digest only once a day. While you're online you may decide to check your e-mail before you log off; that can easily waste precious time.

Perhaps you work on computer networks and have the capacity to remain online all day, so that whenever a new e-mail hits your mailbox, either an alarm rings or the dulcet tones of the "You've got mail!" guy announces a new delivery, and of course what else can you do but check it out? After all, it might be something important.

Yes, it might, but think about all the e-mail you receive over the course of a week. How much of it truly requires you to take immediate action? If the sender really needed your immediate response, after all, she would probably either call you or stop by your office.

Cell phones and pagers are no better when it comes to their loud and urgent demands. Because these devices—like e-mail—have appeared on the scene so quickly and have made an incredible impact on our lifestyles in a relatively brief period of time, a canon of etiquette regarding their proper and polite usage has not had time to form. How often have you seen a person who blatantly abuses the technology—switching on the cell phone at every ring, regardless of whether he's in a fancy restaurant, on a crowded train, or even in the doctor's office—being met with hostile stares and even rebukes from total strangers who may think he's flaunting his high-tech advantage. Or else you walk down a city street where every other person you pass has a tiny cell phone glued to his ear while his mouth is busily talking to the air in a scene straight out some rabid technophobe science fiction flick. Cell phones are similar to call-waiting devices on regular telephones: if you're out in public with a friend and your cell phone rings and you answer it, the not-so-subtle message you're sending is that the person calling may be more important than the person you're with.

Perhaps worst of all, you see the driver in the car one lane over from yours slowly veering straight for a collision with your vehicle because she's deep into a conversation on her cell phone and is totally oblivious to her surroundings. Many states are currently trying to legislate these cellular drunks, with mixed results.

As you would deal with constant interruptions by the telephone and by coworkers, the best way to deal with these high-tech interruptions is to set limits on the amount and periods of time when

SMART DEFINITION

Outsource

This is a relatively new word that has only begun to be used in popular context in the 1990s, as companies discovered it was often cheaper to farm out certain work—whether a one-time project or the entire bookkeeping system—than to retain a full-time employee, with the overhead, salary, and benefits an in-house worker implies.

Outsourcing is the art of pushing certain projects off your plate and onto a person or company who is happy to handle them.

you will respond to them, and inform the people that you are in contact with on a regular basis about your—and their—restrictions.

Outsource It!

Even if you're a dynamo at work, doing the jobs of three people while still leaving the office by five every afternoon, there are still those times and projects where you will be physically and emotionally unable to handle everything yourself. Whether you outsource some of the tasks to another department in your company that you regularly work with, hire another business to handle the extra work, or give it to an independent contractor or a temporary employee, farming out some of your most overloaded projects can be the best time-management step you can take.

You learned about the art of delegation back in chapter 2. Outsourcing particular tasks and responsibilities is taking delegation one step farther. Remember, the ideal tasks to delegate—and therefore outsource—are those that don't require the special talent or outlook that you bring to your job. Grunt work and routine tasks are good tasks to farm out at first; then, if the job comes back well done, then you can make the next task you assign a little more challenging, and so on.

A growing number of companies are beginning to outsource such regular and mundane tasks as bookkeeping, computer maintenance, and even payroll, particularly in the case of small firms where these tasks were being performed by employees who were hired for another purpose. If you were assigned these tasks in addition to your regular duties, and would prefer to spend your time doing what you were hired to do, it may be worth your while to investigate what it would cost to outsource them. You—and your boss—may be surprised to discover that outsourcing entire departments will actually cost the company less than if you were to hire staff to perform these duties in-house. Admittedly, not every company or boss will be amenable to letting go of the reins, but it may be a good idea to start to train some of your higher-ups to see how they can benefit if they outsource and/or delegate even a few tasks, or allow you to find someone to handle the additional responsibilities.

Once you have done your research into the costs and schedule, try to sell your boss on the idea by playing up the positive: "If I can outsource the accounting and bookkeeping tasks to an accounting firm, that will free up my schedule enough so that I can finally help you get going on the new marketing campaign that you've been wanting to start for months, but that neither of us have had the time for."

Or words to that effect. If you're planning to outsource some tasks, here are some things to keep in mind:

• Realize that you'll need to make arrangements to outsource work at least a month before you'll need it. In other words, if you wait until you've reached the absolute breaking point and the project in question needs to be done yesterday, you will lack the time and the clarity to thoroughly research the choices that are available to you. For instance, if you've been assigned the responsibility for making sure the floor in the front reception area is cleaned and waxed regularly, and it's a job you usually enjoy doing but you haven't done it for more than a month and an important client or prospective customer is coming to visit the office, don't call a cleaning service on the day you need it or you'll be out of luck.

• If it's up to you to make the decision about the tasks that can be outsourced to lighten your workload, ask yourself three questions: Will another person be able to pay more attention to the task than I can? Will s/he be able to do it faster? And does outsourcing this task mean that I will save money, considering what my time is worth? If your answers are yes to even one of these questions, then feel free to proceed.

• Make sure you have the opportunity to clearly spell out the task(s) you wish to outsource as well as the deadline for their completion. If the deadline is written in stone, make that clear at the outset. Make sure that the person or business knows to come to you with any questions and to keep you updated with regular progress reports about the project. Finally, ask for and give feedback when the project has ended.

Keeping On Top of Supplies

If you've ever run out of copy paper in the middle of an important copying job, or your laser printer ran out of toner and you rushed to the supply closet for a replacement only to find there were none left, then you know how important it is to make sure that supplies are always kept at sufficient levels in your office. And if you're currently the person designated to keep track of office supplies, among a million other responsibilities, this may be a good first task to delegate to one of your coworkers, so that you can be freed up to concentrate on your other work. In fact, if you have outsourced your office cleaning duties to an outside cleaning service, you may ask them if they can take care of maintaining and replacing the office supplies as well.

Whether you're the one responsible for keeping an eye on the supplies or you're able to farm out the duty, here are a few ideas to help streamline the task as much as possible:

• If you have the storage space, buy supplies like paper, printer toner cartridges, and mailing supplies in bulk through the mail. Not only will they tend to be less expensive on a per-item basis, but you'll also save lots of time since no store visit is necessary.

• Most office-supply companies will gladly send a salesperson to visit your workplace every two weeks or so to go over your stash of office supplies and replenish the ones that are low or out of stock. You can also tell her about any special items that you think you'll soon need. She'll then arrange for the supplies to be delivered to your office, in most cases, the next day.

• Schedule a time each week to check on the supplies to see which are running low and which need to be reordered. Do this regularly, on the same day and at the same time every week so that you are not caught short.

SMART SOURCES

Warehouse office supply stores carry just about everything, but sometimes you'll need a special paper or notebook for a project or occasion. Turn to one of the smaller specialty supply companies. Here are a few:

Paper Direct

Features unique paper that can run through your printer for elegant invitations and other correspondence.
800-A-PAPERS
www.paperdirect.com

Artlite

Offers a wide variety of unusual pens and writing instruments. Check out their Pen School online.
800-327-PENS
www.artlite.net

Mobile Office Outfitter

If your vehicle has turned into a second office, check out this source for handy gear.
800-426-3453
www.mobilegear.com

• Determine which are the busiest times of year at your office, when you tend to go through a lot of supplies quickly, and make sure that you keep these special occasions in mind when you check the supplies on your weekly timetable. You may want to order twice the regular quantities right before these hectic times of the year.

Needless to say, just dumping your new boxes of toner, envelopes, pens, and paper into an empty closet without any thought to arranging them won't save you much time in the long run. If they're not organized into some kind of order, you may not notice when you're running low on a particular type of colored copy paper your boss likes, or you may order too many pens because you didn't see the three boxes that had fallen onto the floor behind the box of copy paper.

Consider buying a freestanding supply closet if you don't have enough room to stock your supplies, or add some extra shelving to a hall closet. The important thing to keep in mind when arranging your storage space is to create an area where you can tell at a quick glance where you stand on supplies. That means you don't want to bury boxes of paper clips behind larger boxes. If you group similar items together, in much the same way they're arranged in an office supply store, you won't waste time searching for items.

While you're organizing your supply storage area, you'll want to clean out old supplies and items that you no longer use, or that have dried out, or that don't fit your new printer or copier. Be ruthless when you scour your shelves and desk drawers: when you see that old computer manual, that handful of old pencil nubs, or those rusty paper clips, ask yourself if you could ever see using the item again. And even if you could possibly use it, would it send the wrong message to the companies and colleagues you do business with? After all, you don't want to jeopardize your relationships and future work with other businesses: if in doubt, throw it out!

Managing on the Road

Keeping your life organized and running smoothly when you're at the office is hard enough. If you travel frequently on business, the organizational mess can easily get compounded and it can become much more difficult to stay organized and stick to your new and still-fragile time-management resolutions.

While technology has made it almost ridiculously easy to stay in touch with the office, it has also produced some unexpected ramifications: After all, it wasn't too long ago when it was understood that a business trip afforded the traveler a chance to get some well-deserved rest and relaxation. That expectation has been shot out the window with the bevy of electronic devices that allow people to contact you no matter how far away you are.

Even if you manage to get away from your office workload when you are on the road, you can still get as much work done as you would at home—perhaps even more, since you can learn to view all that time when you're stuck on airplanes or spending late nights in hotel rooms as a welcome chance to get some of your quiet work, or creative thinking, done. After all, think of all the

SMART SOURCES

As the volume of business trips has increased in recent years, companies have sprung up to help make corporate travel easier for both the traveling employee and the company. Here are a few:

• Trip Mastr is a checklist that will help prevent you from leaving an important item behind. Champion Publications 800-238-4809

• *The OAG Pocket Flight Guide* (North American edition) is a monthly subscription that provides the times and dates of every flight from every airport in the United States. Veteran business travelers use it to reschedule canceled flights.

• Magellan's is a mail-order company that specializes in luggage and travel accessories. 800-962-4943 interruptions that you will be bypassing back at the office!

Travel provides a plethora of situations that can stress you out and waste your time. In this instance, attitude definitely is everything, and a positive outlook can mean the difference between a wretched travel experience—which can also spill over into the business meetings you've scheduled for your trip—and a chance to advance your company and your career, take advantage of some downtime, and even talk with people you would never have met if if you weren't both in transit.

With this in mind, here are some time-wise travel tips to help keep you sane and healthy and in control of your time when you're on the road.

• Set aside a time each day when you're incommunicado, and people back at the office will know they won't be able to get in touch with you. Endless phone calls from coworkers can be horrible distractions when you're trying to prepare for an important meeting the next morning.

• Wrap up as many projects as you can before you leave on your trip, and make sure that other projects you're in the middle of can be put on hold while you're away.

• Don't feel you have to know every little detail about what's going on back at the office when you're not there. After you get back, you'll find out what you missed soon enough.

• Do a thorough check of your business trip inventory the night before you leave. Make a list of the items you will need for your trip, and then check them off the list as you pack them away. Arranging to have something sent overnight when you're in a hurry is not only expensive but it will wreak havoc on your nerves, possibly spoiling your meetings and presentations the next day.

• At the same time, you're not a camel, so you don't need to bring everything that you might possibly need on your trip. Do you really need your laptop, palmtop, portable fax, cell phone, and the other electronic devices you use every day? Cull out those you think you won't use or can easily find substitutes for. Fax machines and other electronic devices are readily available in hotel business suites and airport lounges.

• If you're on the road because you're on vacation, enjoying some badly needed downtime, do yourself a favor and contract a severe but temporary case of amnesia when it comes to the work back home. Yes, there are certain people who find it impossible to relax and not think about work when they're supposed to be on vacation, but getting away from it all and destressing your brain during the time you spend in a new venue will do more than anything else to spark your creativity once you get back to the office.

From dealing with your boss to keeping on top of supplies, it may frequently seem like managing your time and your office is just one big balancing and juggling act. It tests your strengths and weaknesses in ways you probably had never expected. In fact, it might just seem easier to throw in the towel and become a hermit than to keep your time-management goals on track.

As it turns out, maintaining your program of time management and organization at work is a

WHAT MATTERS, WHAT DOESN'T

What Matters
• Being polite but straightforward about your deadlines.

• Acknowledging that some interruptions are unavoidable.

• Assigning a priority to every interruption.

• Suggesting ways to reduce the number of interruptions.

What Doesn't
• Believing that your deadline is license to be rude to those who interrupt your work.

• Complaining that you have no control over interruptions.

• Treating each interruption with the same degree of nonchalance or urgency.

• Ignoring the built-in interruptions and not providing ideas for ways to change them.

THE BOTTOM LINE

When you make a commitment to become more organized and time-savvy at the office, you may be surprised to discover that a host of people and factors are out to sabotage your efforts, both directly and indirectly.

If you stick to your guns—and your well-thought-out schedule and neatly organized workspace—your efforts to remain organized won't be thrown off track by an occasional ill-timed interruption or well-meaning coworker who just wants to chat but who is really looking for an excuse to blow off work. Keep your commitment to yourself in mind every day, and you'll be able to keep to your schedule. Remember, the time you save is your own.

piece of cake compared to what you'll learn about next: trying to get your partner and kids into the act at home. After all, at the office, there's a certain set of protocols that employees know they should follow, or risk expulsion. At home, you'll find it's a bit trickier, but your time-management goals are eminently reachable if you learn a few well-placed tricks.

Time Management at Home

It is easier to forego time management and organization at home than it is at the office because, after all, you get paid to keep things in a rational order at work; there's no such incentive when you're under your own roof. In addition, when you're at home you want to relax, and not spend your time doing something that resembles work in any way.

As is the case with managing your time better at the office, learning how to arrange your home life in a more efficient manner will take some planning and extra time at first. But the good news is that after you've laid the groundwork, you'll actually have more time to play and relax than you did in your preorganized days.

The Fine Art of Running Errands

Running errands can run you ragged. How many times have you run out of the house to do your grocery shopping and found when you got to the store you'd left your list at home? Or if you didn't write down certain items, you didn't remember to pick them up? Or you devoted your lunch hour to picking up the dry cleaning and ended up having no time left to eat?

Errands can easily consume a good chunk of your spare time if you don't adequately plan your course of attack in advance. The key to spending a minimum of your time running errands involves several steps:

• Reduce the number of stops you have to make.

• Purchase items before you need them, and buy in bulk whenever possible.

• Try to plan a workable schedule and try to plan key events to occur at the same time each week.

Here are the details:

Reduce the Number of Stops You Have to Make

Giant shopping malls, huge department stores and supermarkets, outlet centers, and one-stop convenience and discount stores that are open twenty-four hours a day have served as lifesavers for many harried people who have too many errands to run and too little time in which to do them. Despite the prevalence of these retail outlets in most parts of the country, many people still regard them as just yet another store to visit, and not as a lethal weapon in their plan of attack in the war against errand proliferation.

If, for instance, you are familiar with the toy aisle in the chain department store but haven't visited any other part of the store, set aside some time to stroll the aisles the next time you're there. How many items do you see on the shelves that you buy anyway, but at other places? How do the prices compare? If they're similar or less expensive, your choice is made for you. Making one stop instead of several is an obvious time saver. If, however, the item costs more, ask yourself if you're willing to pay the additional expense to save the cost and time of having to drive to another store, fight traffic, find a parking spot, and then wait on line a second time. Think of those people who willingly drive ten miles to save two cents a gallon on

F.Y.I.

If the stores and shopping plazas where you make most of your stops on your errands are spread out and you are not sure of the most direct route, given one-way streets, traffic lights, and the like, call your local AAA office. They'll be able to write a special TripTik for you, which will spell out the best way to get from point A to Point B, even if both points are in the same town.

gasoline. If you're one of them, look at the extra time it takes and the aggravation you develop versus the relatively small amount of money you'll save. Then ask yourself if it's worth it.

Purchase Items before You Need Them, and in Bulk Whenever Possible

You know the types of products you use on a regular basis, or at least those of which you always have at least one package tucked away in your storage closet. Before you head out the door on a shopping errand, or if you've scheduled it for later in your day after work or another planned activity, quickly scan the shelves to see what things you're running low on, and add them to your list.

Plan a Workable Schedule and Try to Plan Key Events to Occur at the Same Time Each Week

Many of us do our errands whenever we can find the time. Of course, there are probably ten things you can think of that you'd rather be doing, so that doing your errands gets pushed off again and again until you reach the point that you *have* to do them because you've run out of supplies at home, or you need a special item for the weekend and it's already Friday night. When you finally do your errands, the roads and stores are crowded, you're annoyed, and when you reach the store, they're either out of stock or closed.

Planning to do your errands at the same time and day each week—preferably at a time of the day when the stores are at their least crowded—will eliminate some of the mad frenzy that usually accompanies your last-minute errands. Plus, it will allow you to think clearly and buy what you need without purchasing too much of one item or forgetting to get something else.

It's also a good idea to plan your stops so you can stop at stores along the way instead of having to backtrack. Again, think of the stores you frequent most often, and the items you usually buy on at least a weekly basis. In your mind or on an actual map, start at one end of the route and work your way through your list of items and stores until you reach the end and you're done. Isn't that easier than making a mad dash from one store to the next, in your haste forgetting an item you must have, and then having to return to a store where you've already been to an hour earlier?

Paying the Bills

It doesn't take a degree in rocket science to figure out that the tasks we put off doing the most for the longest periods of time involve chores and activities that we'd rather not do in the first place. Paying your bills has to be on everyone's top ten list.

Thankfully, in the same way that it's positively affected so many areas of your life, technology has also made it easier for you to take care of your bills and finances. From depositing your paycheck directly into your checking account to automatically deducting the money to take care of the bills that need to be paid on a monthly basis, as long as you inform your bank or credit union who to pay, how much to pay, as well as the day you want it paid, you can put some of your regular bills out of your mind, secure in the knowledge that they will be paid.

Unfortunately, not every company that you do business with on a regular basis is set up to accept

STREET SMARTS

One man hates paying his bills so much that he used to postpone it until the last possible minute.

After paying one too many late fees, he now sets aside one evening a month to get bill paying out of the way. He writes the checks, and seals and stamps the envelopes. He also hates having even one penny of the interest in his money market account go to his creditors, so instead of sending all of his bills out on the same day, he puts them in an accordion-style folder with 31 slots, one for each day. Every morning as he leaves, he checks the number for that date—if the date is December 8, he reaches into the file labeled "8"—and then pulls out any bills in it.

He mails the payment out well before it's due, gets his bill paying done in one two-hour session once a month, and holds on to more of the interest his money earns for him.

automatic payments. For those that aren't, there are a few tactics you can use to make things run more smoothly: of course, they involve a little bit of planning and designing a system, but once it's done, you don't have to spend time thinking about it.

The first way to streamline the process of paying your bills each month is by assigning the responsibility to only one member of the family, or at least assign the responsibility for paying the bills that you are jointly responsible for. This way, there's no question about whether or not a bill got paid or the check was mailed on time, unless he or she forgot. If you're the person responsible, try to keep all bills, invoices, and bank account statements located in one area in your house. This way you'll save time by not having to first locate the items and gather them up before they get paid.

Another way to make your bill paying almost painless is to keep your checkbook records on your computer. This way you can use a personal accounting program like Quicken to keep track of your balances and expenses. With its check-printing features along with your laser or inkjet printer, you can even print out checks and keep accurate records with no problem at all. There's also a program currently being tested by the United States Postal Service that allows you to print out stamps on your home printer. Then all you'll have to do is seal the envelope and drop it in the mailbox.

The best part of using financial software is that it absolutely streamlines the process of gathering your records when it comes time to prepare your tax returns and itemize your deductible expenses. As long as you categorize each checkbook entry with a simple code—for example, "M" for mortgage, and "U" for any utility bill—all it takes is one keystroke and you instantly know how much you spent in any one category during the year.

Most banks now allow their customers access to their checking and saving account balances and perform other banking activities online and over the phone. This means that if you have a question about whether a check has cleared or if you need to transfer money to cover an automatic payment or an ATM withdrawal, you can do it at any time of the day or night.

Streamlining Housecleaning

Somewhere, tucked away in the deep recesses of our minds, is a deep admiration for the Conehead character that Jane Curtin played on *Saturday Night Live* because of what she wore: an apron that loudly proclaimed "I Hate Housework." This declaration, which also turned out to be the title of a best-selling book on the subject by author Peg Bracken, provides a hint about one of the best ways to deal with a household activity no one would ever admit to enjoying: with a little bit of humor. Whether that means listening to a standup comic's routine on CD while you dust and polish—or whatever it is that will keep you smiling and busy—is up to you.

The best way to streamline your housecleaning chores is to keep on top of them as they come up, instead of waiting until your entire house looks like a wreck. Because at that point, you'll either have to spend an entire day—on the weekend, of course—to get everything relatively back to normal, or else lower your standards to accept living

SMART DEFINITION

Tickler system

A tickler system basically tickles your memory once a day, or once a week or less often, so that you remember you have to do a particular task. You can use index cards, file folders, or computerized tickler systems to remind you of important dates and tasks.

amid the clutter that you have allowed yourself to become accustomed to. Keeping on top of chores means that instead of placing a dirty cup or plate in the sink that will eventually end up in the dishwasher anyway, you take the two extra seconds to open the dishwasher and place the cup in the rack when you're already standing at the sink.

Just as you have occasional periods of downtime at the office, you also have them at home. Take advantage of those times when you're watching TV or waiting for a friend to call you back to spend a few minutes to straighten up a room or quickly run a dustcloth over your furniture.

Of course, one way to have a clean house without lifting a finger is to hire someone to do it for you on a regular basis. If you feel funny about paying someone to do something that you feel you should be doing yourself, stop and think: how much would it really cost? And how much is your free time worth? Or better yet, if you can afford to have someone else do the things you would rather not do, think of all the ways you could spend the time when you'd otherwise be dusting, vacuuming, and mopping the floors. Now, isn't it worth it? If you do choose to have someone else do it, you'll be in great company: service businesses—which include maid and housecleaning services—are one of the fastest growing businesses going

Of course, you don't want to take it to the extreme that some people do, and clean the house to make it presentable for the person who comes to clean your house. After all, you already know that you have better ways to spend your time. However, unless you're fortunate enough to have a live-in maid you're still going to have to do some of the housekeeping yourself. Here are a few tips to make it as painless as possible:

• Cleaning is an ideal activity for multitasking, since some housekeeping chores require a bit of time to "work," like cleansers and floors drying. As long as you have the momentum going, go on to another chore while you're waiting for those to finish.

• One quick-and-dirty way to do your housecleaning is to temporarily focus on the areas that people see; in other words, master the art of cleaning at eye level. Why bother cleaning areas that no one will look at anyway?

• Delegate responsibility. After all, why should you do all the work if everyone contributes to the mess?

• Store the items that you use together in the same place, and not too far away from where you will need to use them. This goes for both cleaning supplies as well as specific foods, dishes, and utensils that go together. This way, these items don't get spread out and lost, creating more of a mess than is necessary.

• As you are preparing a meal, if the recipe and your schedule allow, wash the pots, bowls, and utensils as you go. Not only will this fill in the minutes between steps in a recipe, but you'll also save time later in cleanup. And once food has dried on a spoon or mixing bowl, it takes more elbow grease to get it off.

• Keep a basket near the stairs and fill it with all the stuff from one level that needs to be returned to the other level. Every time you go up or down the stairs, take the basket with you and unload it before you put it down.

SMART MONEY

The next time you start to worry that you're not getting done all you should be, think of what time-management expert Mark Sanborn has to say:

"Some things are worth doing well, some things are worth doing very well, and some things are just worth doing."

An appendix: some things aren't worth doing at all, at least by your hands. So if you need to hire another pair of hands to help out around the house, do it.

• To save on cleaning supplies, and to make it more convenient when you start your house chores, store your rags, bottles of ammonia, and cans of cleanser in a portable bin with a sturdy handle. You'll also save time because you won't have to spend extra minutes heading for another part of the house just because you happened to have left a cleaning tool in another area.

The final argument for why you should not get too bent out of shape when it comes to cleaning your house, or worry about hiring somebody else to help you out, is best described by the title of another best-selling book on housecleaning, by Harriet Schechter, that helped readers regard housekeeping with humor:

The title of the book was *More Time for Sex.*

Training Your Kids

You bought this book because you wanted to learn how to manage your time better. When it comes to helping your kids learn the same lessons, well, by now you know from experience that you can lead a kid to the vacuum but you can't make him turn it on.

Most kids are by nature messy and disorganized. A combination of at least twelve years of school, parental discipline, and finally, peer pressure, will bring them to the point where they'll want to look a bit neater, wake up on time—since you've given up on dragging them out of bed each morning—and even straighten up their rooms so they won't waste an afternoon looking for a particular CD or magazine.

The key is consistency. With younger children, the reward system frequently works: "If you put your laundry away, then you can go out and play." But with older children and teenagers who are fully able to pick up after themselves, threats tend to be more effective. With that said, it won't help to criticize their style of housecleaning or to constantly supervise them.

Entire libraries could be filled with books that tell parents how to get their kids to do what they are asked to do and to rear them to grow up to be contributing members of society, and besides, you know best how your kids react to certain orders. In the meantime, to help your kids learn how to manage their own time better, and to help keep the entire household from falling behind, here are a few tips:

• Face it: kids take longer to clean up than you do, and they probably won't do it as thoroughly as you do. If you're not already familiar with this fact, now is the time to confront it.

• Do as many of the household chores as you can together, as a family. Not only will the chores get done sooner, but you can use the time as family time when you can chat with your kids, talk about school, plan where to go on your next vacation, and so on. Working together can also make necessary chores seem almost fun.

• If your kids are in the prekindergarten stage, start training them early to help pick up after themselves. The bonus is at this age that kids actually like to help a parent to work around the house. Remember, as long as you're not too picky about how it looks or how they get it done, having your

SMART MONEY

Azriela Jaffe, the author of several small-business self-help books, has the art of managing kids and work down to a science, even though they both occur in the same place: her house.

She has been called "the queen of multi-tasking," because of the seemingly impossible amount that she gets done each day. Here's her secret:

"I segregate my workload into four categories: Do now; Do while baby is with the babysitter; Do when baby is under my care; and Do when family is in bed. And, I frequently do two things at once. For instance, I save such silent tasks as folding laundry for when I'm on the phone. If a friend is coming over, I'll visit with her out in the garden while I'm picking tomatoes.

"The key is to maximize every moment of the day."

One man who shares custody of his two young children with his ex-wife says his kids are normally pretty conscientious about keeping their rooms neat, but lately they've gotten sloppy and forgetful. The reason is that the two parents have two very different ideas of what cleanliness is. "When they first arrive at my house, they're throwing things all over the house," he reports. "By the time they're ready to head back to her house for the next week, they're back to keeping their rooms picked up. But then they come back and it's back to square one."

One thing he did was to tell them anything left out on the floor was going outside. After this happened a couple of times, their memories improved and they only needed an occasional reminder.

kids help even a little bit will mean less work for you, and more time for your other interests and activities.

• No matter how neat you'd like the rest of the house to be, make sure that every kid has a place to call his own where the normal rules don't apply. Whether it's a corner of his room or the basement, or a spot in the backyard, it's important that each kid has a space that he can control however he likes. This should make him more willing to keep up with the rules you set for the rest of the house.

• To help make sure that your child has time to help you around the house when necessary, buy him his own datebook so that he can keep track of his own appointments. More schools are now requesting that students maintain personal calendars, and the best part is that it frees you from having to keep yet another datebook.

• Get a family message center that combines a calendar, a bulletin or message board, and storage bins to keep keys, school handbooks, and other essentials from getting misplaced. Make sure you place it near the door that you use most often so everyone will see important reminders or dates.

• If your kids tend to forget to give you important school notices—permission slips that need to be signed or reminders that you need to deliver twenty-four cupcakes to the school the next day—give them minicassette recorders to carry around with them. Explain that any time they need to tell you something, they can say a few words into the tape recorder, and then be sure to play it at the end of each day.

• Make sure you remain alert to the possibility that your kids have too many activities in their schedules. Oh, they'll probably find an excuse to say they're too busy to help out with chores around the house, but if your daughter would really benefit from having her own secretary or chauffeur, then it's a good bet that she has too many things to do, both in school and as extracurricular activities, and that you both need to decide together about the best places to cut back.

Training Your Partner

In our multitasking, dual-role society where everyone is used to doing more than one thing at the same time and where fathers are supposedly as comfortable with child-rearing responsibilities as women say they are with being the family's primary breadwinner, most men and women in relationships or marriages are used to pulling their weight. In many families, each partner takes responsibility for one part of household maintenance—from mowing and raking the lawn to paying the bills—and although some weeks will find one or both of them behind on their particular chores, they are still generally in agreement about the fact that they both need to pitch in to keep the household humming along.

But what happens when you and your partner share radically different thoughts of what effective time management, neatness, and household cleanliness mean? Do you good-naturedly grin and bear it, or do you grit your teeth and do more than what you feel is your fair share while the resentment seethes and builds inside you, after

F.Y.I.

A recent study at the University of Washington found that husbands and male partners who take on an equal share of the housecleaning tasks are generally both emotionally and physically healthier than men who let the women do all the work. So the next time your guy starts to balk when you hand him a mop and pail, tell him to do it for his health.

spending long months or years trying to get your partner to change?

It's not uncommon to hear that the issue of combining two radically different styles of time management—or mismanagement—and neatness standards has served as the final straw that broke up a relationship that had probably been on the verge for a while. While some partners are able to appreciate their differences and let some things go, understanding that their partner is able to tolerate some personality quirks that another less open-minded individual would view as just cause for World War III.

If you're in such a partnership and fall halfway between these two extremes of tolerance when it comes to your partner—sometimes his slovenliness bugs you no end while at other times you're able to totally overlook it—you probably have a live-and-let-live attitude; in many otherwise equal relationships, the good balances out the bad and both partners learn to expect that.

However, there are a few things you can do to get your partner to change the habits you occasionally find intolerable without your partner's even knowing what you're doing. And by the way, you can follow the same advice when it comes to getting along with the people you work with in other areas of your life—at the office, at your place of worship, and in your social organizations.

• If your partner tends to run late to meetings and social engagements while you're punctual to a fault, tell him that the appointment is a half hour earlier than it actually is. This way, if he tends to run fifteen or twenty minutes late, he'll actually show up early or on time. For this tactic to work, however, your partner should have a decent sense of humor about his or her failings; otherwise, your partner may take offense at being lied to when you were only trying to help.

• If your partner tends to be a pack rat while you try to throw out everything the instant you think there's the slightest possibility you'll never again use it, some compromise is in order. Agree that your partner can hold on to most of his or her stuff if he or she at least puts it into some kind of manageable order. Of course, this may result in your loved one stuffing everything he or she owns into a spare room just to get it out of your line of sight, but accepting that solution would be your end of the compromise. Your partner might just ask for your help in getting organized if he or she tries to stuff even more junk into the room, but finds that the door won't open.

• If you are the more detail-oriented of the couple, while your partner employs a more seat-of-the-pants style, try switching roles. Exaggerate what you feel are your partner's negative habits, and stage an elaborate game of charades, but with the volume turned way up. Offer your beloved a legit chance to explain his or her approach and why he or she thinks yours doesn't work. Then reverse the scenarios. Throughout it all, try to maintain a sense of humor about your diametrically opposed styles. In fact, during this exercise you may feel like you're acting in a particularly raucous Marx Brothers movie, but sometimes a combination of humor and truth is the best way to get at the heart of the matter and understand the other person's motivations and reasons for behaving in a certain manner.

WHAT MATTERS, WHAT DOESN'T

What Matters

• Getting your family to pitch in around the house whenever possible.

• Making sure you pay your bills on time.

• Running your errands in a timely fashion while covering the most direct route.

What Doesn't

• Acting like a dictator just because your family's standards are not up to yours.

• Obsessing over every penny of interest you lose when you pay a bill early.

• Sticking to a particular route when running your errands because "that's the way it's done."

• Learn to compromise after having an honest discussion about your differences. What bugs you most about the way your partner is different from you when it comes to managing his or her time and cleaning the house? Do you feel your partner is being inconsiderate of your feelings when he or she leaves clothes strewn all over the floor as if expecting you to pick them up? And does your loved one feel you should mind your own business and take care of your own things and not worry about how he or she treats his or her own possessions? Some easy compromises would certainly make a huge difference. Your partner could agree to restrict clothes-dumping to just one room in the house while you could learn to overlook your partner's housecleaning style as long as he agrees to spend an hour on Saturday morning helping you to clean the house.

In the end, you'll find it will improve your home life immeasurably if all the people living under your roof don't take themselves too seriously. You and your family should be able to accept that other family members will probably not be able to meet up to—or down to, as the case may well be—everyone else's standards. Although it's a wonderful thing to live in a relatively clean and organized household, the world won't come to an end if something's out of place. What matters is that you make the time to be together and that you're not so stressed out that you don't enjoy that precious time.

Both high-tech tools, such as personal finance software, and low-tech helpers, like dustcloths cut from old Mickey Mouse pajamas, work wonders when it comes to keeping on top of your organization and time concerns around the house. And the best motivation to involve your family is the old carrot on a stick approach.

But what measures do you take to stay on top of the game? From home to the office, what can you do to ensure that these newly learned good habits stick? For the answers, turn to the next—and final—chapter for lots of the inspiration that you'll need.

THE BOTTOM LINE

With all the chores that await you at home, it may seem like it requires lots of skill to keep the management of your time and space from turning into your second full-time job. It helps if you can learn to not take it seriously, and get over the idea of clinging to certain white-glove standards.

But perhaps the greatest key to successful time management at home is to learn to view it as a chance for your family to spend some time together and to have fun doing it. Throw in a few rewards, allow everyone the freedom to express their own style, and you'll be well ahead of the game.

Staying Ahead of the Game

Wow, you're almost there! The fact that you have managed your time well enough to reach the last chapter of this book, given all the other things competing for your attention, shows that you're one fast learner.

But you know how it can be with most self-improvement books: You learn a little bit about how to do a few things better, and actually start to integrate a few changes into your life. But before you know it, real life interferes and you find yourself sidetracked. And within a few days you have enough trouble keeping track of what you need to do tomorrow, let alone trying to remember how you're supposed to be doing things differently. You know the rest of the story: once you return to your old ways of doing things, your good intentions fly right out the window and you're back to square one.

The good news is that since time management involves everything you choose to do, if you change one little thing about the way you do things—arriving five minutes early all the time, for example—it will quickly become a habit. After all, managing your time is easy; it's keeping time from managing you that's difficult. The tips in this last chapter should help you to hold onto everything you've gained. You have nothing to lose except wasted time.

You Time

By taking the time to read this Smart Guide, you have learned about the many ways you can free up more time for your work, your family, and even your social responsibilities. But there's one thing missing, and it is one of the primary reasons why people get cranky when they have an overbooked, though well-managed, schedule:

They forgot to make time for themselves.

Everyone needs a little time for him- or herself, whether it is to read a book without interruptions, take a yoga or dance class, or go out for an aimless drive through the country. Think about the last time that several weeks passed while you made sure there was enough time to do things for your boss and your family, but when it came to finding the time to do something you wanted to do, somehow there never seemed to be any time left.

So what happened? You probably found it was tough to drag yourself out of bed in the morning, you snapped at coworkers, friends, and family for no reason, and you began to feel unchallenged and unmotivated.

Interestingly, doing only for others without taking care of yourself usually causes the same emotional side effects as going too long without taking a break from work. It is hard to get motivated—even by work that you used to jump out of bed in the morning for—when your brain feels stale and the same four walls feel like they're closing in.

As with other aspects of improving your time-management skills, if you want to have some time for yourself when there are so many other activities vying for your attention, you have to take a proactive stance to consciously work it into your schedule. And if you think you don't have time to fit it in, ask what you can give up. Be ruthless. After all, you can't be helpful to other people unless you are treating yourself right first. Think of the advice that flight attendants give about the drop-down oxygen masks during the preflight safety instruc-

SMART SOURCES

Here's a simple way to get to *you* time: set an alarm clock for the time you need to move on to the next activity. Instead of a typical ringing or buzzing alarm clock, try a gentle vibrating alarm clock that you can wear against your hip and that will allow you to gradually make the transition.

A good place to get a gentle alarm clock is Brookstone, which has hundreds of retail stores across the country, a thriving mail-order catalog business, and a Web site. In addition to purchasing a gentle alarm clock, you'll be able to find lots of other products to help you manage your time more effectively while pursuing your dreams.

Brookstone
800-926-7000
www.brookstoneon
  line.com

tions: adults should take care of themselves first so that they're better able to help their children.

So if you feel guilty about taking the time for yourself when you could be doing all these wonderful things for everyone else in your life, learn to regard your personal time as a way to help your family. Think about how refreshed you feel after taking a break to do something you enjoy: you were able to temporarily forget about your problems, to stop worrying about what other people need for a short time, and, most important, to totally indulge yourself in an activity of your own choosing. Don't you feel ready to face the world again after indulging in these small luxuries?

Here are a few ways to create the time for yourself, with no more excuses:

• Change your work schedule in some way—by working from home, by going to work early or late, or by working part-time instead of full-time. Even as little as one day a week can make a difference to free up the time you need to do what you want to do.

• Get everyone out of the house on a Saturday afternoon, and then luxuriate in being alone. Try not to set any goals or plans for your time alone; just do what comes to mind. Watch a movie no one else ever seems to be in the mood to watch, putter around the kitchen, or just sit and stare out the window.

• Jealously guard your time alone. This means letting the answering machine or voicemail pick up all calls and not answering the doorbell if it rings. In fact, stuff a sock in the door chimes and turn the ringers off all of the phones in the house.

Now is the time to warn you about a little-known side effect that may develop as you begin to organize your life. Once your spare energy is no longer consumed by hunting for lost papers or running from one errand to another in a highly inefficient manner, guess what? You'll have more time. And while that time may be quickly filled by work or leisure activities, you'll probably be able to think more clearly, which will eventually cause you to ponder what you really want to do in your life.

It may not happen immediately, and it may be very subtle. But inevitably the subject will come up. After all, if you were able to accomplish the monumental task of getting your life and schedule organized, what will you be able to do next?

Take a Break!

Or better yet, a vacation. As you've just read, the symptoms of going too long without personal time for yourself are similar to those of working for too many weeks and months without taking at least a few days to not do anything that in any way resembles work.

However, if you work at home even part of the time, getting a break can be tough to accomplish. After all, there's always at least one project that could benefit from some of your attention. Even housework can distract you. Here are a few ideas to help you to take a break.

• Set aside one full day a week—that means twenty-four hours—when you pledge not to do a stitch of work.

• Get out of the house! Gather everybody together and head out on a day trip with no agenda and no schedule. Just go!

• Enlist everyone in the decision as to where to spend a vacation. This may be difficult since many of us have passed along the concept of our family vacations to the next generation. As a result, at least one family member is usually unhappy with the current plans: keeping to a schedule, visiting places deemed to be educational but that end up boring everyone to tears. It's time to get out of the principle of "This is a family vacation and you're going to have a good time whether you like it or not," and end the cause of millions of lousy child-hood memories with your generation. It may mean compromise, it may mean five different trips, but just do it.

Once you begin to take more regular vacations, you may discover that you want to incorporate more breaks into your life, every day. While you probably won't want to quit your job—unless you start your own business; see the next section for details—you may want to consider downsizing your position. You may find that your job doesn't quite fit your priorities the way it used to. You've changed, and you may want less work but more of the freedom and extra time you've come to enjoy so much.

If you're happy with your company and they've been pleased with your work, you might approach your boss about switching to another job in the same or a different department. Maybe you want less responsibility and/or fewer hours. Though some of your coworkers may look at you in wonder, you should maintain that this is what you want for yourself. It doesn't matter if you're making less money or carry a less prestigious title. If it is possible to create a new position, combining the best of your current job responsibilities with some new ones, maybe you could pass some of your old duties on to a colleague or assistant. After all, if you're happy, the company will benefit as well.

Managing Your Time While You Start a Business

If you want to start your own business, the first thing you should know is that you're in great company: more than 75 percent of Americans believe that the key to happiness and success is to run their own business.

When it comes to time management, the best thing about running a business is that every day is different. If your modus operandi at your current job is to count the minutes until you can leave, once you start your own business, you simply won't have time to watch the clock. In the same vein, the worst thing when it comes to time management and running your own business is that, yes, every day is different: your life as an entrepreneur will be filled with extinguishing lots of little fires over the course of your day, so that when it's time to go home—which is usually much later than the hour you skip out with at your current job—you may look back at the day and wonder just what exactly have you accomplished.

STREET SMARTS

Despite the stories you hear about entrepreneurs working a hundred hours a week, there are exceptions. Jim Hoskins runs Maximum Press in Gulf Breeze, Florida. He reveals a truth about how the type of business you choose will directly influence the amount of time you devote to it.

"Nothing is more valuable than your time," says Hoskins. "If you make a lot of money and have a successful business but no time left over, you lose. The ideal is to have a business selling products, but not time, because time is more valuable than money. If I'm selling a product, it'll live its own little life while I'm not working. If I'm a dentist, if I'm not working, I'm not making money."

"Pick a business that positions your lifestyle the way you want it to be," he says.

When that time comes, however, you'll just have to reread this Smart Guide. To get to that point is another story. Because going into business—any type of business—is filled with all kinds of risks. Not only because you're investing your time and money in order to get your venture off the ground, but also because once you start a business, it frequently will take on a life all its own, one that may well diverge from what you envisioned when you first started out. And when it comes to derailing some of your time-management goals—particularly those goals related to your personal life—the sheer hours and attention that a new business frequently demand from its founder are enough to tempt even the most stalwart boss to return to those previously disorganized but familiar ways.

However, because you are the boss, you can call the shots, within reason. You have the power to decide exactly how you want to run the company. If you want to run your business in a particular way—from your home and/or on a part-time basis, for example—then plan for it and just do it. If you don't want the burden of having employees of your own, you can plan for that as well. Fortunately, with a little bit of control, attention, and foresight, it is possible to shape the kind of business you want.

Although there will inevitably be those times of the year when your business will be consume every free moment, it's important to keep reminding yourself that you can plan for it and decide how to handle it when the time comes. It's quite possible that once you have your business up and running, a particularly delicious moment for you will be when you will have to refer back to the *Smart Guide to Managing Your Time* to see how life is lived on the other foot: for example, if you need to hire some extra help but don't want to take on a regular employee, check back with the section on outsourcing in chapter 6.

Move to Paradise

. . . Or at least what you regard as your own personal view of paradise. Many people who live in congested, traffic-jammed cities and suburbs think of a small town or a rural village as paradise with open space, fresh air, friendly people, and room to live.

While living in a country town does give you more control over your life—and therefore your time—it is not a panacea: most of the problems you have in your life while you're living in your current crowded domain will follow you even if you move to a small town. However, you may feel better equipped to deal with them once the crowds, congestion, and time-wasting pursuits are mostly gone from your life.

If you don't feel like you're ready to go completely rural, you might first try going beyond the suburbs but not to an overly rural area. The new *exurbia* is a way to experience a new way of life without having to give up some of the things that are familiar.

No matter what you choose, moving to the country usually involves more than just a change in venue. It's about changing your entire life. That's why it's important to get real about why you want to make this change in the first place. The first step is to deal with the fact that you are leaving your seemingly secure, known life behind you. However, are you moving *to* a place where you know

F.Y.I.

In 1997, more than six out of every ten rural counties in the United States gained population, reversing a decades-long (in some cases century-long) slide. A total of 2 million people moved from cities and suburbs to small towns in 1995.

you'll be happy, or are you only mulling over the idea of moving because you'll be moving *away* from your current home and all of its aggravations? If your primary reason for leaving is because you hate your current life, you're moving for the wrong reasons. If, however, you can be realistic about what your life will be like, and how you're going to spend your days, and you're willing to go through the learning curve and accept that there will be some parts of rural living that you probably won't like, then you're more likely to stick it out in the sticks.

If you're serious about moving, ask yourself the following questions. By the way, you can also apply these questions to any other life change that you are thinking about. Whether that means taking up horseback riding or committing to read one book every week, your answers will lend some insight into your motivations.

1. Why do I want to move to the country [or wherever]? Write down five answers and rank them in order of importance.

2. When do I want to move? Now, or when is a more realistic time and date?

3. What do I want to know how to do after I've been living in the country for a year? How will I go about learning it?

4. How will I spend a typical day living and working in the country.

5. What is my fantasy rural house and its setting? Is it in a village, ten miles out on a dirt road, or somewhere in between?

6. What do I like about my current job?

7. What do I hate about my current job?

8. What do I want to learn in the process of preparing to move?

9. What is one thing that I could do today to bring myself one step closer to moving to the country?

10. What's my biggest excuse for not moving to the country?

What's Holding You Back?

Okay, so you've dutifully read almost every page of the *Smart Guide to Managing Your Time,* you've purchased a wealth of organizational tools, from fluorescent Post-it notes to heavy-duty filing cabinets to a new datebook, and you've plotted out your plan of attack for how to deal with your partner and your kids.

All right, so what are you waiting for? Why are you still hesitating?

We all know that change can be difficult. Fair enough. But why wouldn't you want to start improving your life immediately?

Ask yourself this question: If all of the excuses that are preventing you from starting to manage your time better were taken away, would you still do it? Or would you frantically start looking for more reasons why you feel like postponing what may be a radical overhaul? You've gotten this far, and you know what you need to do. What is swirling around your head?

• This is selfish.

• This is so out of character for me.

• What if I don't like it?

• What if I like it *too* much?

• How will this change my life?

• What if I don't succeed?

In addition, you may be nervous about the possibility of changing and you may feel scared about the prospect of not being able to return to your previous life. Plus, at this juncture, you may have no idea what you will gain from it. You should take heart in knowing that you're not alone. Especially if you've never had to organize your life or physical space before, paying this much attention to a part of life that you've up to now ignored or haven't put much faith in may seem absolutely alien to you.

Or it's possible that you may be afraid of what you'll become. If you're an extremist at heart, once you have your life in order you may start to go off in the other direction and consider yourself superior because of the things you learned and what you were able to accomplish from putting a few time-management tools to work for you. Try not to get preachy about your transformation; as the cliché goes, people will get it if you live by example.

What it usually comes down to is telling yourself it's okay to do it, in essence, to give yourself permission. It may help if you can talk to a few people who have experienced a similar drastic change in their lives, or have even gone from being a total slob to the queen of space and time management. People in twelve-step programs have mentors they rely on for advice that's sincere, because it's given from an "I've been there" perspective. Who says you can't have the same kind of support network?

In the same vein, getting your life in order may turn out to be one of the biggest adventures of your life, simply because it is so different from anything else you've ever done. True, there will always be a reason—or a hundred—to prevent you from proceeding with your plans to manage your time. But you have to learn to just ignore all the negatives and start to totally change your orientation. Act as if you already are the most organized person in the world. At this point, some people will have to admit that they just are not up to it. But the first thing you have to do is to make up your mind that you are going to do it, and everything else will surely follow.

Time-Management Checkup and Troubleshooting

After you have had a chance to institute some of the time-management exercises and projects into your life, it's time to give yourself a checkup. It is a good idea to evaluate your experiences and the areas where you have met or exceeded your goals,

SMART MONEY

Neil Bull is the director of the Center for Interim Programs, in Cambridge, Massachusetts, which helps overtaxed college students and executives take a break, and then pursue what it is they really want to do.

"There's so much in our society that tells us not to make a move, and people throw up many barriers at the same time. Because it's so alien, it takes time to marinate about the things that you want to do, and then plan things so you have no choice but to make it happen."

In the course of your research you may have uncovered another dream that you didn't know you had. The important lesson is to trust your instincts. If one part of your time-management plan doesn't quite fit, let it be. You may come back to it later, or you find something more suitable.

"Getting people to uncover what they really want to be doing is like working on a jigsaw puzzle," says Nella Barkley, cofounder of the Crystal-Barkley Corporation in New York. "The first pieces that appear don't really make much sense in the beginning, but later more of the picture starts to emerge."

She adds that it's difficult for people to know exactly what they want to do because their real desires have been so submerged after years of being and acting the way that other people expect them to be. She first directs her clients to identify the things they most want to do with their lives. They then narrow it down, working out a timetable and then fill in the details as the plan starts to emerge.

as well as other areas where you would like to do a little better.

The purpose? To see what is working and what isn't, to adjust your work and home styles accordingly, and to decide whether you want to continue working with these changes for the foreseeable future. A close analysis at this stage will help you to focus more of your attention on the areas where you feel that you fall short, or to concentrate on expanding the facets where you've succeeded in getting organized to other parts of your life that could use a little more management.

Performing this analysis now will also help you to decide how you're going to change your time-management style from this point on, that is, if you feel that you need to add any changes at all. Take some time to answer the following questions in as much detail as you want:

• Do you feel that you've accomplished your main time-management goals? How so?

• List the five best things you have learned about yourself so far as a result of managing your time better and organizing your life. How can you use this information?

• List five things you wanted to do, but didn't. How would you change your day-to-day schedule so that you could place more priority on them?

• What are the things you want to do differently from now on, if anything? What do you want to remain the same?

• And what are you going to do now with what you have learned?

Failure is one of the hardest things for most of us to admit to—but what if the extensive plans, all the new technology, reconfigured schedules, expensive datebooks, and other tools and plans you worked on for so long somehow aren't working the way you had imagined? Should you keep plodding on and hope that things get better or should you cut your losses?

Of course you know that reading about new ideas that sound like they could dramatically change your life for the better and getting fired up over them is frequently half the battle. But once you start working to integrate these changes into your daily life, it may not turn out the way you expected. You start to lose your enthusiasm, you let a few things slide, and then you figure what's the use.

Wait a minute. Most people have had a project they worked on that didn't quite live up to their expectations. In many cases, they tried to figure out what went wrong, and then got back up and tried again from a different angle. After all, many of the ideas and strategies presented in the *Smart Guide to Managing Your Time* are tried and true, but sometimes people first have to tweak them a bit in order to fit them into their own lives and situations.

When it comes time to evaluate your own time-management strategy, you should take the same approach. The first thing you have to do is determine where things have gone awry. Ask yourself the following questions:

• Did I overschedule or underschedule my time?

• Did I expect too much?

• Did it take me so long to get used to managing

my time and getting better organized that it took me a while to hit my own stride?

• Did I decide to start managing my time better based not on my own desires, but somebody else's? Or did I do what I thought would be good for me, instead of what I instinctively knew would truly work for me?

If any of your answers indicate that you need to revamp your daily routine, then do it. Sometimes people who are in the process of changing their lives get so excited about it that they go at it wholeheartedly and then get burned out and disillusioned by the resulting onslaught of sudden change, before leaving it all behind and returning to what's familiar.

The entire process of learning how to manage your time better requires that you take a broader look at yourself, and recognize both your strengths and your shortcomings. So if you're having trouble, it's especially important to quickly evaluate what's gone wrong so you can hold on to the positive changes you've made and which have worked for you, while retooling your approach where you've fallen short. The only thing that really matters is what works for you, so try to be open-minded and reactive when evaluating any problems or setbacks you encounter over the course of getting more organized.

Changing Your Habits

Over the course of this book, you may have nodded in recognition at some of the bad habits that are described, and perhaps even agreed with many of the time-saving and organizational tips mentioned. You also may have thought about the time-management skills to incorporate into your life, planned it out, set aside the money to do it, and begun envisioning yourself living a more organized, peaceful life.

But there's still one thing left that you haven't done: actually start.

Some people are able to take drastic measures in stride and make them part of their everyday lives. Either their time-management project is only one of the more radical in a long line of risks that a person takes, or it's the first-ever high dive, which makes everything after that seem simple. However, even though you've made up your mind that you're definitely going to take the plunge, it doesn't necessarily mean that your mind is going to be totally comfortable with the idea.

It's a big step, stepping away from the security of the disorganized, mismanaged life that you've always known. Here are some tips if you still have cold feet:

1. Pretend that your new time-management commitment is a new job. Your first day of work is the target date you've set to start organizing your life; all you have to do is report for your first day of work.

2. Do people think of you as steady and predictable in your messy ways? It's always fun when

STREET SMARTS

If you want to change your life, you need to be patient. Lionel Carbonneau is a very patient man.

In 1972 Carbonneau was working in sales and ten years away from retirement when he began planning his retirement business: an antiques shop run from his barn in South Barre, Vermont. He started to build his inventory by buying from individuals, knocking on doors, and buying from shops.

In 1983 Lionel and his wife, Marilyn, opened The Country Loft Antique Shop, filling the barn with all of the antiques he had collected through the years.

When it comes to starting a business or making any major lifestyle change, Carbonneau has two pieces of advice: "Crawl before you walk, and love what you're doing. Otherwise, you're going to get stung."

people suddenly get a picture of you as an entirely different person. Let this drive you toward your goal.

3. Ask yourself if you'd really be happy continuing to live as you are. (A tiny part of you must be dissatisfied if you picked up this book in the first place.)

Overcoming Resistance

We're creatures of habit. We become used to living under a certain latitude and living conditions, and we balk if we're asked to change. But when the change is self-initiated, that's a different story. Then, once you become comfortable with this change, it becomes difficult to change yet again, and on and on . . .

Overcoming the resistance of your friends, family, and coworkers can be the most difficult challenge of all. What can you do to overcome this resistance? The primary effort should be to show these people that you intend to stay committed to your work and previous goals; the only thing that's changed is the method in which you've chosen to accomplish your work. You can actually pitch it as a benefit to everyone around you: once you become more efficient in your tasks, your work takes up less of your time and you have more time for your family, coworkers, and other interests.

You may be surprised to discover you may encounter a backlash against your new habits. After all, your increase in efficiency may make them look lazy and indifferent by comparison, and they might be incredibly jealous and resentful of what you've been able to pull off. The best thing to do is to gradually win them over to your side, pointing out the benefits—more time for your personal interests, for one—and easy ways they can start to employ some of the same time-management and organizational tips that you've integrated into your life. In fact, serve as their mentor. Ask them what they would do if they had an hour or two more each day to spend as they wished. Bring them through the steps that you took, and give them time to realize that they can free up a good chunk of their time as well. Help to make them aware that even though it's scary, they should take the chance, because the rewards are much greater than the risks.

What's Next?

After you've had a chance to allow your new time-management program to settle into your life, it's a good idea to look back and evaluate the changes in your life, for better and for worse. Look at the areas where you've met or exceeded your goals as well as the other areas where you would have liked to do a little better.

Why should you take the time to evaluate your progress? To see where you excelled and to analyze those areas where you could have done better, while developing a clear picture of the reasons why. This will help you to give more of your attention to the areas where you think you fell short, or to decide to just ditch the ones that just didn't take and to concentrate on the things that you enjoy most and do best.

So be honest and answer the following questions in your notebook in as much detail as you feel you need:

1. Do you think you accomplished the main goals of your time management program? How was this done?

2. List the five best things you learned from managing your time better, and then describe how you learned them.

3. List the five things you didn't learn but wanted to. How could you have arranged your life differently in order to place more priority on them?

4. What would you have done differently, if anything? What would remain the same?

5. What are you going to do now with what you've learned?

Although you know you're living a different life and the benefits are very clear to you, sometimes it's very hard not to slip back into your old, sometimes destructive habits. How can you prevent this from happening and still retain all of the good habits you've developed?

First, take the answers you wrote down to the previous questions and look at the list of things you've gained. If it helps to make a sign and hang it up at work or home, or put some reminders in a place so that they're never more than an arm's length away, then do it. This will help you to be aware of the times when you're slipping, a mental rubber band of sorts around your brain when you find yourself doing or saying the kinds of things that caused you to pick up this book in the first place.

But don't walk around with a chip on your shoulder because you've made some gains in managing your life and time better and those around you haven't. In other words, don't get preachy. As the cliché goes, people will get it if you live by example.

In the end, of course, and what we tend to lose sight of in the mad rush we seem to be caught up in, is that you are in control of your life, and it's up to you to make it what you want it to be. Learning how to manage your time better is a great way to start to turn your life into the one you really want to be living.

No one says it's going to be easy, however. If you think you have too many choices now, the first thing to realize is that it's not going to get any better. In fact, the onslaught of information and options will just grow with each passing day. That's why it's more important than ever to learn how to control your time today since there will be more things than ever to distract you from your true goals.

After all, time will never slow down for you; and if you think that you can wait for retirement to take it easy, answer this: after a life filled with intellectual activity and frenzy, do you think it is even remotely possible for you to "take it easy"? If you're anything like the rest of us, it will be highly unlikely.

Accept your fate; but first take the time to learn how to use your time better.

Congratulations! You've made it! From learning about some new, relatively painless ways to get your

WHAT MATTERS, WHAT DOESN'T

What Matters
- Listening to how other people have managed their time.

- Reassuring yourself at a temporary setback, and getting back on track.

- Knowing that sometimes you'll try too hard, and recognizing that not everything works for everyone and moving on.

What Doesn't
- Trying a new time management trick even though it won't work for your situation.

- Being hard on yourself because you've temporarily reverted to your old bad habits.

- Continuing to work at a new method or technique when it's clear it's not a good fit.

THE BOTTOM LINE

Time management is not all about keeping to an inflexible schedule or squeezing more activities into a longer day. It's more personal than that: once you learn how to use your time more effectively, you'll begin to think about the ways in which you're filling up that time, learning which to hold onto and which to let go, as well as discovering new activities to pursue.

Whether you end up working less, working more, or just spending more time on the kinds of things that make you feel happy, this is what effective time management should mean for everybody.

life under control to actually starting to use them, you've taken some giant strides toward feeling more satisfied with your life.

Now that you've attuned yourself to the benefits of effective time management and can see concrete ways in which your life has changed, you're probably starting to think of other ways to organize your life even more—the advanced course, so to speak. When these ideas pop up, pay close attention because it's your intuition giving you a direct line to additional time-management tips that are as close to a perfect fit for you as you can get.

Now that you're well on your way to shaping your life into your ideal as well as moving toward your dreams, keep going. Just be sure to make time to pat yourself on the back for a job well done.

Appendix

Use the following forms, checklists, and worksheets to help you to begin managing your time better. Make photocopies of those you'll use most often.

Weekly Planning Guide

The Five Most Important Tasks This Week:

1._____

2._____

3._____

4._____

5._____

Action Plan

Necessary Tasks to Complete Goal	Necessary Resources	When to Begin?	When to End?

Weekly Schedule Planner (by the half hour)

Hours	Monday	Tuesday	Wednesday	Thursday	Friday	Saturday	Sunday
6:00 AM							
6:30							
7:00							
7:30							
8:00							
8:30							
9:00							
9:30							
10:00							
10:30							
11:00							
11:30							
Noon							
12:30							
1:00							
1:30							
2:00							
2:30							
3:00							
3:30							
4:00							
4:30							
5:00							

Hours	Monday	Tuesday	Wednesday	Thursday	Friday	Saturday	Sunday
5:30							
6:00 PM							
6:30							
7:00							
7:30							
8:00							
8:30							
9:00							
9:30							
10:00							
10:30							
11:00							
11:30							
Midnight							
12:30							
1:00							
1:30							
2:00							
2:30							
3:00							
3:30							
4:00							
4:30							
5:00							
5:30							

Weekly Schedule Planner (by the hour)

Having a daily planner can be useful, but sometimes plain is best, so that you're not distracted.

	Morning	Afternoon	Evening
Monday	7 8 9 10 11	12 1 2 3 4	5 6 7 8 9
Tuesday	7 8 9 10 11	12 1 2 3 4	5 6 7 8 9
Wednesday	7 8 9 10 11	12 1 2 3 4	5 6 7 8 9

	Morning	Afternoon	Evening
Thursday	7	12	5
	8	1	6
	9	2	7
	10	3	8
	11	4	9
Friday	7	12	5
	8	1	6
	9	2	7
	10	3	8
	11	4	9
Saturday	7	12	5
	8	1	6
	9	2	7
	10	3	8
	11	4	9
Sunday	7	12	5
	8	1	6
	9	2	7
	10	3	8
	11	4	9

Time Tracker

Project	Starting Time	Ending Time	Total Time	Activity

Project Task Planner

Use this to make a list of all of the necessary things you need to do to break down your projects into manageable tasks. For example, if you need to publish a company newsletter, you'll have to determine the story ideas, find writers, locate photographs, layout the design, contact the printer, and then distribute the copies.

Project I	Project II	Project III	Project IV

Priority Planner

Separate all of the work- and home-related tasks you need to accomplish in the course of a month into one of four categories. If, by the 20th of the month, it looks like it's going to be impossible to accomplish the remaining items on your list, try scheduling fewer tasks the following month. You may be overly optimistic about the number of tasks and projects you're able to fit in over the course of one month, let alone twenty-four hours.

Important Urgent	Important Not Urgent	Less Important Urgent	Less Important Not Urgent
Work:	Work:	Work:	Work:
Home:	Home:	Home:	Home:

Energy Tracker

Use this chart to make a list of your tasks and projects, both at home and at work, and then rate each task as to the amount of mental and physical energy that's required to complete the task, as well as the time of day that you'll be at your peak to work on it. Rate each task from one to five, with one being very taxing and five requiring very little in the way of energy.

Tasks and Projects	Mental Energy	Physical Energy	Ideal Time of Day

Travel Planner

Sometimes when you travel, it's the unexpected things that can eat up your whole day. Keeping track of your goals and needs while you're on the road is one of the most important things you can do to make your travel worthwhile.

Person to See	Purpose of Visit	What Do You Need for the Visit?	Expenses
			Travel: Hotel: Meals: Misc:
			Travel: Hotel: Meals: Misc:
			Travel: Hotel: Meals: Misc:
			Travel: Hotel: Meals: Misc:
			Travel: Hotel: Meals: Misc:

JANUARY						
Sunday	Monday	Tuesday	Wednesday	Thursday	Friday	Saturday

FEBRUARY						
Sunday	Monday	Tuesday	Wednesday	Thursday	Friday	Saturday

MARCH						
Sunday	Monday	Tuesday	Wednesday	Thursday	Friday	Saturday

APRIL						
Sunday	Monday	Tuesday	Wednesday	Thursday	Friday	Saturday

MAY						
Sunday	Monday	Tuesday	Wednesday	Thursday	Friday	Saturday

JUNE						
Sunday	Monday	Tuesday	Wednesday	Thursday	Friday	Saturday

JULY						
Sunday	Monday	Tuesday	Wednesday	Thursday	Friday	Saturday

AUGUST

Sunday	Monday	Tuesday	Wednesday	Thursday	Friday	Saturday

SEPTEMBER						
Sunday	Monday	Tuesday	Wednesday	Thursday	Friday	Saturday

OCTOBER						
Sunday	Monday	Tuesday	Wednesday	Thursday	Friday	Saturday

NOVEMBER						
Sunday	Monday	Tuesday	Wednesday	Thursday	Friday	Saturday

DECEMBER						
Sunday	Monday	Tuesday	Wednesday	Thursday	Friday	Saturday

Index

Books in the
Smart Guide™ Series

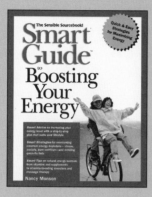
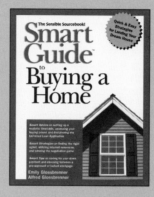

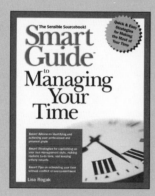

Smart Guide™ to
Boosting Your Energy

Smart Guide™ to
Buying a Home

Smart Guide™ to
Getting Strong and Fit

Smart Guide™ to
Getting Thin and
Healthy

Smart Guide™ to
Healing Foods

Smart Guide™ to
Making Wise
Investments

Smart Guide™ to
Managing Personal
Finance

Smart Guide™ to
Managing Your Time

Smart Guide™ to
Profiting from Mutual
Funds

Smart Guide™ to
Relieving Stress

Smart Guide™ to
Starting a Small Business

Smart Guide™ to
Vitamins and Healing
Supplements

Available soon:

Smart Guide™ to
Healing Back Pain

Smart Guide™ to
Maximizing Your
401(k) Plan

Smart Guide™ to
Planning for Retirement

Smart Guide™ to
Planning Your Estate

Smart Guide™ to
Sports Medicine

Smart Guide™ to
Yoga